Set the Standard

Most of us know the *tactics* for creating cultural excellence, but we sometimes struggle with motivating our teams to make real and lasting changes. Chris York melds together both pieces in this impactful book. *Set the Standard* is proof that the way to move the needle on big results is to focus on the people at the bedside while creating an inspiring environment where all actions are grounded in love. He covers foundational building blocks, such as an emphasis on feedback, true employee ownership, a continuous change mindset, reward and recognition, and caring, respectful language—and uses incredible storytelling to bring these concepts to life.

—**Quint Studer**, author of
The Calling: Why Healthcare Is So Special

This inspirational book offers tenets to drive excellence in organizational performance, beginning with "love one another." While there may be those who think that this principle is trite, one of the world's most profound healthcare thinkers, Avedis Donabedian, expressed similar views over a half century ago: "Ultimately, the secret of quality is love. You have to love your patient, you have to love your profession, you have to love your God. If you have love, then you can work backward to monitor and improve the system." York's book, *Set the Standard*, extends Donabedian's concepts via the pragmatic chapter section "Leadership Lesson" that can be deployed immediately to improve organizational performance in healthcare and across other business sectors.

—**David J. Ballard**, MD, FACP, MSPH, PhD, MBA;
past President of the International Society for Quality in Health Care (ISQua); Adjunct Professor, Health Policy and Management, at UNC Gillings School of Global Public Health, University of North Carolina at Chapel Hill

Set the Standard is about a journey of character, compassion, and optimism about the soul. I had the privilege of hiring Chris York fourteen years ago because he walked the walk of being a leader of character. I remember thinking that this was a man who had the gift of seeing an associate's potential more than the associate could realize. Chris has a God-given talent for enabling organizations to reach their maximum potential through engaged teams. He cares deeply about associates, patients, and community, and this is vividly reflected in his book *Set the Standard*. Chris describes excellence through stories designed to capture the heart and motivate the reader to more excellence than he or she thought possible. In fact, excellence is a manifestation of loving others. Throughout the book, Chris describes situations that helped him cultivate the raw potential of employees toward the goal of ministering to others. *Set the Standard* can change the way you think about work, teams, and ministry if you take the time to read it!

—**John B. McWhorter**, DSc, MHA, BS;
Chief Operating Officer, OhioHealth

Compelling, insightful, vulnerable, inspiring, and *real*—that is how I experienced this fascinating book on leadership. In *Set the Standard*, Chris York uses a storytelling format to teach leaders how to choose excellence over mediocrity. He calls for you to become more than you think you can be and then hands you the blueprint to your own leadership success. As he shares the vivid details of his leadership journey, it is as if you are sitting right next to him at the fireplace and he is answering your questions before you can even ask them. His examples are so easily understood and remarkably relevant that one would be embarrassed to ignore his advice of building a culture of love. I have read many leadership books in my lifetime. *Set the Standard* is hands down the most impactful and pleasant read I have encountered. It will leave you motivated, smiling, and a better person in all aspects of your life.

—**Beth P. Beckman**, DNS, RN, APRN, NEA-BC, FAAN; Chief Nurse Executive at Yale New Haven Health System; Associate Dean of Clinical Partnership at Yale School of Nursing

What makes *Set the Standard* different than many others on healthcare leadership is Chris York's passion and deep commitment to the belief that, for him, healthcare is a calling, and it is indeed his ministry. I have had the privilege of knowing and working alongside Chris as a peer with the same healthcare system for more than seven years. One of the hallmarks of his leadership is his intentionality. Each day he heads to the hospital in search of opportunities to make a difference in the lives of physicians, nurses, patients, and fellow team members. Within our system, Chris is one of the leaders who truly sets the standard for exceptional, caring, and servant leadership. It is an honor to know him and call him friend! His book, *Set the Standard*, is filled with practical advice for all of us who are always wanting to up our game and take our leadership skills to the next level. Whether you are in the midst of taking on your first leadership role or you are a seasoned healthcare leader, Chris provides practical steps to growing your leadership skills beyond average to becoming an exceptional servant leader.

—**Glenn A. Robinson**,
Fellow, American College of Healthcare Executives

CHRIS YORK

SET THE STANDARD

THE ANTIDOTE TO AVERAGE

NEW YORK

LONDON • NASHVILLE • MELBOURNE • VANCOUVER

Set the Standard

The Antidote to Average

Published in New York, New York, by Morgan James Publishing. Morgan James is a trademark of Morgan James, LLC. www.MorganJamesPublishing.com

Proudly distributed by Ingram Publisher Services.

ISBN 9781631958793 paperback
ISBN 9781631958809 ebook
Library of Congress Control Number: 2022930591

Cover & Interior Design by:
Christopher Kirk
www.GFSstudio.com

To my loving wife (Jackie) and son (Jack),
You are a constant source of love and inspiration in my life.
Each of you sets standards of excellence
in your own lives and in ours collectively.
I love and admire you both more than words can express.

CONTENTS

FOREWORD

"Why get out of bed to be average?"

With this one riveting question, award-winning hospital president Chris York offers a life-changing challenge to thousands of leaders and caregivers: Set the standard! Don't be average, for *average* is just another word for mediocrity. Make no mistake: Chris is not inviting you to simply beat the average. He is daring you to *set the standard* of excellence that every patient seeks, every caregiver hopes for, and every mission statement promises.

Why this book now? Because healthcare leadership has lost its way. Consumed by budget worries, corporate red tape, and day-to-day demands, leaders have taken their eyes off the reason hospitals exist: to deliver loving care with high competence and deep compassion.

Chris knows that leadership teams can sail to the top if they awaken untapped energy and aim for excellence. In fact, I have heard him say many times: "Perfection is impossible. We aim for it anyway. In doing that we achieve high-level excellence by living love every day and night. Love is in our DNA."

Serious questions arise in this masterful book: Are America's hospitals engaging in leadership malpractice by tolerating "average" care for those deeply in need? How much better could caregivers perform if leaders engaged the most powerful and most underutilized energy we know: love?

Chris understands that love as a leadership strategy has been ignored because its power has been underestimated and its practices have been misunderstood. To this day, some are baffled when he explains the success of the hospitals he has led: "We are loving leaders, and we are leaders who love leading." What does that mean? Chris answers that question beautifully in his powerful book.

For two decades I have watched Chris emerge. As president and CEO of Nashville's Baptist Hospital System in the late 1990s and early 2000s, I spotted him and told our chief operating officer, "Chris York could be a spectacular CEO if he finds two things in his heart: passion and belief—a passion that leadership is his calling and a belief that he can do it." Twenty years later, after helping two different hospitals rack up one award after another, he was named Healing Hospital CEO of the Year. Across forty years during which I was fortunate to lead three different hospital systems to the top and to author the best-selling *Radical Loving Care*, I learned to spot the best. I know this with confidence: Chris York has set a new standard and has met it. He is one of those rare beings who lives his faith and loves his wife and son. Love is not something he saves for work. It is a gift from God that he lives every minute.

Tomorrow morning do not remain in bed comforted that you are better than average. Rise up and set your own new standard! Chris York is doing that because he knows that patients, caregivers, and God are counting on him. They are counting on you as well.

The Reverend Erie Chapman, MTS, JD
President, Erie Chapman Foundation, Nashville, Tennessee
Founding President and CEO, OhioHealth

THE ANTIDOTE TO AVERAGE

Why get out of bed to be average? Does anyone dream of being an average leader? Does any organization aspire to be average? Of course not! Yet, by definition half of any population is average to below average. Do not let it be you!

Have you ever wondered why some people experience great success while others struggle or, worse, accept mediocrity as a way of life? Sadly, organizations are filled with people who accept average performance.

Set the Standard is a guide to leadership. It's about setting the standard at whatever it is you do. Through it you'll learn how to maximize your potential and that of your team. The following pages will create a pathway to increasingly higher standards—if, that is, you are willing to take the journey. Those who are unwilling to put in the work will inevitably find themselves mired in mediocrity—not a place you want to be.

Setting standards requires more than just effort. It requires us to create cultures so thirsty for excellence that anything short of the target is immediately rejected in pursuit of a never-ending journey for something better. It requires cultures that provide the reward of purpose in what we do so that each new day brings with it an energy around new opportunities.

Setting standards also provides great rewards in the form of satisfaction, knowing you are in pursuit of something special and finding yourself elated over seeing others engaged in the pursuit of the extraordinary. Setting standards through hard work also brings joy and gratification in knowing you have made a difference in the life of another person, knowing you are expressing love through your work as well your personal life, and knowing your customers are being cared for through high competence and deep compassion.

Every day, each of us are presented with options: get out of bed thirty minutes early to workout or sleep in; limit yourself to five minutes on social media and spend fifty-five minutes doing yoga and meditation; spend an hour scrolling through material for momentary entertainment; go over to meet a new neighbor; crash on the sofa with a movie. So many options. Are your selections leading toward excellence?

This book invites you to engage in thrilling processes and choices by caring for others through leadership. We all lead in some fashion—formally, informally, titularly, or organically. How can you use your influence to create a better world around you?

Beyond inspiration, this book provides proven methodologies on how to lead, how to develop other leaders, and how to take your team to the next level.

Is there a next level? How do you get there? Unless you are a one-person show living on an island, the insights and experiences in the coming pages will offer proven strategies that not only transform companies but, more importantly, the lives of the people who comprise those companies.

What makes leadership exciting and rewarding instead of being just a job? As a leader, there are few better experiences than seeing people grow, experiencing team development, and watching customers be delighted in the process. Through the coming pages and the work thereafter, my desire is that you will be challenged and encouraged on your leadership journey, and that you will become a blessing in the lives of those you touch along the way.

As a leader, you are a standard bearer. Be the person who searches for more, who seeks new heights. When everyone else is satisfied and complacent, be the inspiration to climb the next hill, to fight the next battle. Be the person who displays the discipline, who conveys the commitment, and who provides the perseverance to *set the standard.* It will not be easy, but it will be incredibly rewarding. There will be times when you will wonder, *Are my efforts worth it?* or *Am I making a difference?* Hang in there! This book, through real-life examples and proven techniques, will help answer those questions with a resounding yes! All the while impacting people in a way that enables them to become better workers, team members, spouses, parents, and citizens. A better life for you and those you lead is not just attainable but sustainable if you challenge the existing standard, and, more importantly, set higher standards as a part of your leadership journey.

The impetus for this book came from colleagues who had experienced this work firsthand. After finding joy in the environment and, more importantly in their work, these friends and co-laborers in setting standards would periodically suggest, "You should write a book about this work." Initially, I dismissed the thought. After repeated suggestions from a variety of leaders, I offer the following in hopes of encouraging others along their leadership journey.

1
THE GOAL

Life is either a daring adventure or nothing at all.
—Helen Keller

Why get out of bed each day to live an average life and do average work? Are you instead energized by the pursuit of something seemingly unattainable? I am. As a child on the smaller side, I dreamed of playing college football and did. As a mediocre student, I found a passion for learning and went from reading books as punishment to writing one. Finally, for the pinnacle of pursuing the unattainable, look no further than my lovely wife. People tell me that when we married, I outkicked my coverage.

Do you find mediocrity to be offensive, or has its insidious nature lulled you into acceptance? Sincerely reflect on that question.

Regardless of your role or industry, excellence is the only goal worth pursuing. The good news is that if you desire excellence, there is nothing stopping you from creating an environment that breeds excellence: where people love the process of achieving it; where people live it; and where love is demonstrated to all involved through the process itself. I am fortunate to be excited to get out of bed each day in pursuit of a passion for creating the best possible environment for healthcare workers and all the patients we serve. However, that did not happen overnight. Over time, I learned and applied proven strategies and tactics that transformed two local hospitals into nationally recognized organizations, both in a relatively short time frame. These efforts consistently improved the entire environment while making top-notch metrics a by-product of the process. And they not only transformed organizations but also lives.

Setting the standard begins with organizational culture and ultimately allows us to set the standard in every aspect of life. In what follows, I offer a process that converts ancient wisdom into a contemporary causeway. It is the practice of *loving leadership*, an approach to awaken what great leaders always do—bring out the best in others.

Getting Started

For more than a decade early in my career, I walked two paths: hospital-based management engineering and youth ministry. It turned out that these two disciplines had stunning symmetry. Many would suggest, and I would agree, that working in healthcare is a form of ministry. Both hospital work and youth ministry aim to support, care for, and encourage others; both flourish when driven by a sense of servanthood and selflessness.

As I began my career in healthcare, my focus in the industry was on time and motion studies, systems design, and performance improvement projects—basically working with clinicians to figure out ways to eliminate the barriers that stood between them and easily delivering high quality, compassionate care. Within four years, I was blessed to work in every department of a large hospital in Tennessee. This was a phenomenal learning environment that gave me a behind-the-curtain understanding of the entire hospital. This experience also helped me realize that there are two types of people. The first group is *engaged*. They love what they are doing and love giving their best. Excellence is their aim as soon as their feet hit the floor each day. The next group is a mixture of people who are, for one reason or another, *disengaged*. They are fine with the status quo; average is acceptable. To stratify this second group, some might argue there are three groups of people: the engaged, fence straddlers, and the disengaged.

In my experience, however, I've found that there is excellence, and then there is everything else—no matter how many shades it may come in. The group of people not committed to excellence spend their days going through the motions, resigned to accepting mediocrity. Any passion they may have once held for excellence has been beaten from them by leaders who were ill equipped to lead. The system made it easier for them to default to something no patient or customer would ever want—average performance.

A primary goal of leadership should be to equip, support, and ultimately convert this second group to become high-functioning and fully engaged team members. This is where my second career path came into play.

When not at my day job, I spent the evenings and weekends working with high-school-aged youth. This experience helped me gain a deeper appreciation for how much better we, as a society, should be related to loving and caring for one another. We can become so preoccupied with our own lives that we miss daily opportunities to demonstrate love and care for those around us. I so loved this work that on three occasions I tried to leave healthcare altogether to become a full-time youth minister.

For several years, I approached my day job as a business, dealing with supplies, work processes, customer interactions and outcomes, and the like. My work approach was very mechanical. My evening and weekend role, however, was quite different. There I was focused on the fun ministry of mentoring young people. For the first eight years of my career, I maintained a fairly good separation of church and business. It was in the eighth year that I met one of the two great mentors in my life, the man who wrote the foreword for this book, Erie Chapman. At the time, Erie was serving as the chief executive officer of the Baptist Health System in Nashville, Tennessee. He was and remains a very ministry-minded executive. Fortunately for me, he saw ministry potential in a business-oriented young man.

A Defining Moment

Earlier in my career and our marriage, my wife and I suffered a miscarriage during our first pregnancy. This experience was life-changing in many ways. There was obvious grief, but up until this point, my wife and I had never really needed to access our healthcare benefits since we were young, healthy people. Interacting as a customer with the industry I worked in was eye-opening. I will never forget the compassionate nurse and doctor who, while attending to my wife's obvious needs, took a moment to simply ask me, "How are you doing?" My response was, "I'm fine. Thank you." But in my head I was thinking, *My wife is the patient. Why are you asking me how I am doing? Focus on her.* Both of their interactions caused me to pause and realize how much I was hurting. Their compassion enabled me to appreciate what an amazing opportunity we have through daily interactions to be kind and thoughtful to those around us. It also demonstrated how simple gestures can make a big difference in the life of someone who may be hurting.

This doctor and nurse never stopped caring for my wife, and they played a vital role in providing real-life examples of how often we have opportunities to care for and demonstrate love to others. Their actions modeled a great leadership lesson: love is the most powerful force in the universe so figure out how you can use it. They did not have to inquire about my status, but they cared enough for another human being to do it anyway.

There is a difference between providing technically accurate care and actually caring *for* someone. The ability to simultaneously master both is the difference between being good and continuously setting a higher standard.

During this time, Erie Chapman was mentoring me—something he still does to this day—around the ministry of healthcare. I use the word *ministry* intentionally. It conveys the fact that we have countless opportunities to touch the lives of others in impactful ways. The nurse and doctor who reached out to me with simple gestures of kindness and thoughtfulness are a shining example of what it means to take advantage of opportunities to care for others.

The challenge we all face is creating an environment and a mindset that prioritizes these opportunities and demands we seize moments to encourage others. Many of us start our days with a to-do list. That list never has a checkbox for "interruptions." Nonetheless, if we become adept at watching and listening for opportunities to go beyond the requirements in a job description and take advantage of these moments, we begin to weave a beautiful tapestry on which more beauty is created through human interaction. This little extra is an entirely discretionary account anyone can tap into. It remains the challenge of leadership: How do we create an environment informed by love where people *want* to engage that discretionary capacity with each interaction?

As we build the ideal environment, the uniquely beautiful part is our work becomes less like work and more like a calling to do something bigger than ourselves and be part of something that is special. This is where people come alive, where culture is born, and where expectations are set and exceeded because we are routinely capable of so much more than most of us ever dream. Most people just need a small spark in the right environment to become a roaring fire. That, in part, is what leadership is about—creating that spark in others, connecting people to something special, and weaving teams together so that a year or two down the road you look back and see an ordinary group of people who have accomplished the extraordinary. This is done through loving leadership, which includes loving the process of leading.

LEADERSHIP LESSON

Never underestimate what you can accomplish with the right desire and discipline! Ordinary people do extraordinary things every day as a result of working through the process that synthesizes desire and discipline.

The concept is remarkably simple: It is execution that determines what you will accomplish. Nonetheless, each day presents us with endless possibilities. We must actively choose to seize as many of those opportunities as possible to create a better world around us.

To demonstrate the principle of achieving outstanding results through long-term discipline, I encourage you to begin a daily journal listing three to five things you did each day that were not required but made a situation or relationship better because you took the initiative to seize the moment. Over time, you will see how seemingly simple actions can generate incredible outcomes. Going through this process will also make you keenly aware of opportunities to create excellence that you otherwise might have missed.

2

EXCELLENCE: THE ONLY OPTION

Perfection is not attainable,
but if we chase perfection we can catch excellence.
—Vince Lombardi

Life is so much more fulfilling when spent in the pursuit of some lofty, challenging goal. This process of chasing a lofty goal can be broken down through the following sage advice:

> Watch your thoughts, they become words;
> watch your words, they become actions;
> watch your actions, they become habits;
> watch your habits, they become character;
> watch your character, for it becomes your destiny.[1]

The type of building blocks we lay each day determines the type of house we live in throughout our lives. Just as importantly, daily building blocks shape the house or legacy we leave for those who come after us.

My two brothers and I were born into a hardworking, blue-collar home. We grew, killed, or caught much of our own food, and we cut firewood for much of our heat in the winter. Our father obtained a sixth-grade education while our mother made it through the eighth grade. Later as an adult, she obtained a general education diploma. While our father had very little formal education, he was incredibly bright and possessed a work ethic second to none. A tenacious work ethic was one of the greatest lessons he imparted to us. To this day, I remain grateful for the difficult manual labor on hot summer days of cutting firewood, working roofing jobs, landscaping, and serving as general labor on local farms doing whatever needed to be done. All of these jobs provided great life lessons.

While hard work was a mandate, academics were not a priority in our home. If I brought home Bs, I felt like the second coming of Albert Einstein. Sadly, that did not happen very often. And even worse, it was okay not to excel academically.

My First Great Mentor

In our family, no one had ever obtained a college education. Graduating from high school was sufficient. My plan was to finish high school and join the military, which I believe is one of the greatest callings a person can answer. Along the way, I fell in love with the game of football. I was good at it, but not what you would call a blue-chip prospect. As a freshman in high school, I stood five feet seven inches tall and weighed one hundred pounds soaking wet. We used to joke that if I turned sideways and stuck my tongue out, I looked like a zipper.

Stature aside, during this time I met the first of two great mentors in my life. One of these was our high school principal and head football coach, Mr. George Rise. He was a hardworking, no-nonsense man who grew up in the steel mill town of Latrobe, Pennsylvania. Coach Rise always told any student who would listen, "You need to get a college education. It will change your life." Most of the students to whom he spoke were coming from a similar background as ours. We had no real concept of the doors that education could open. I will never forget the extra hours he invested in my life, pushing me to do just one more repetition with one hundred and twenty pounds on the bench press in a small, dingy, high school weight room.

As my body grew and became stronger, so did my mind. I consider Coach Rise the most influential person in my life because he not only challenged me to better myself; he also showed me the way. Through Rise's great coaching and the incredible work ethic instilled by my father, I became good enough to earn a football scholarship upon graduation from high school. Coach Rise, using countless hours of instruction, mentoring, and an oblong piece of leather, planted a seed in me that highlighted the actions of taking pride in what you do, working hard, and being disciplined. Those three intertwined steps will consistently produce the best you have to offer.

Purpose and Passion

Why not set a higher standard for life? My life's goal is to now allow the seed planted by Coach Rise to flourish and continually bloom as a blessing and encouragement to those I encounter, and that includes you.

Throughout, this book plants, repeats, and nurtures the same life-changing question: Why get out of bed simply to be average? Keep asking yourself that question as part of your quest for excellence. There is so much more life to be lived on the other side of discomfort if we are willing to take the first step. If you are in an average rut in life, figure out something else to do. By all means, *stop accepting average*! There is an old saying, "The only difference between a grave and a rut is about five feet." Going with average will only deepen the rut you're in. You can leave this world an average Joe or Jane, or you can pioneer your way out of the rut and into a life that really matters.

How can you live a life of genuine significance? Begin by eliminating the mundane activities that clutter your life and instead feed your purpose, your reason for being alive. Sadly, our world is filled with mediocrity and accompanying time-wasting distractions. Feed your purpose and live a life that is truly alive and passionate about seeking and setting higher standards.

If you are trying to define your purpose, begin by asking yourself a few simple questions:

1. Where do I find meaning in life? This is your passion.
2. What skills and abilities do I have that would be useful in those areas of meaning?

3. Given my passion and abilities, how can I make life better for others? How can my abilities provide a solution to challenges others experience in life?
4. What can I begin doing today that will allow me to focus more time on this intersection created by my passion and skills and some life challenge?

Several things fuel the desire to be great at whatever you set your heart, mind, and hands to do. Primarily, you must love or learn to love what you are doing. Some days that will come easily. Other days, choosing to love what you are doing may require new ways of thinking, even a new mindset about life. Anyone who has ever accomplished something great in their field has made major sacrifices to reach new levels. They have pushed through periods that were more of a grind than glory. Those are the days that build character and forge excellence into expectations.

Living Proof

My wife and I have one son, Jack, who happens to be a living example of this process. At the ripe old age of ten, like his father and uncle had done before him, Jack set a goal to play college football. Through middle school and high school, he made immeasurable sacrifices to achieve his goal. We could not begin to count all the training hours he logged.

At age ten, being bigger than most of his peers, he asked, "What does it take to be a good lineman?"

I told him, "You obviously need a big body, but you also need quick feet."

He replied, "What can I do to get quick feet?"

I encouraged him, "Start jumping rope as often as you can." I provided him a workout to follow at his choosing.

In addition to jumping rope as a workout and through his own initiative, he kept a rope in our living room. Anytime we were watching television as a family and a commercial came on—this was before we had a DVR—he would jump rope during the commercial, eventually creating a worn spot in the floor where he would jump.

In middle school, his youth pastor, John Earle, was a former NFL offensive lineman. At Jack's request, the three of us would get together on Thursday evenings to work on Jack's technique. I simulated the defensive end and could tell right away what many other kids would come to appreciate: Jack had one heck of a punch!

At the dinner table, Jack challenged us to eat better, cleaner meals that fueled his body and ours. Before and after school, on weekends, and certainly during the summer, Jack could be found in the weight room, on the track, or on the field developing his skills while others were still in bed or enjoying their favorite video game.

He started out hoping to receive at least five scholarship offers. His first offer came immediately after his sophomore season. His head coach and former NFL coach and quarterback Jon Kitna had prepared a video to share with the team. As he opened the team meeting that morning, he congratulated Jack on receiving his first offer. He then asked how many members of the team would like to receive a scholarship to play college football. Every hand in the room went up. He then played a video of Jack working out, studying film, and working on his agility. In each instance Jack was alone putting in extra work—no coaches, no teammates, just Jack, his goal, his discipline, and a tremendous amount of work to be completed. As the video concluded, coach Kitna told the team, "If you want to be a college football player, be like Jack York!" As coach walked out of the room, Jack was on the bottom of a dogpile of teammates congratulating him.

For his extraordinary efforts, he earned thirty-three scholarship offers. He ended up receiving at least one offer from each of the major conferences: The Big 10, SEC, ACC, Big 12, and PAC 12. He did all of this while taking care of his academics to the point of receiving invitations to attend the following Ivy League schools: Brown, Columbia, Harvard, Pennsylvania, Princeton, and Yale.

If you are wondering how to start this process, begin by defining a goal you want to achieve. Then set small goals for yourself that, when accomplished, will support the larger goal. There are a number of goal-setting processes. Ultimately, you must create a plan that will allow you to stay focused on milestones that will lead you to achieving your goal. Continually reassess, by asking, *What is my long-term objective?* Through discipline and hard work, you will be amazed at what you can accomplish.

Above all, be committed and be obsessed. There will be too many obstacles to count. The only things you control are your attitude and your effort.

We each need to figure out what it is that makes us want to be great. After a love for what we do, our attitude determines how great our outcomes will be.

You may have heard the old parable of the bricklayers. Once there were three bricklayers. Each one of them was asked what they were doing. The first man answered gruffly, "I'm laying bricks." The second man replied, "I'm putting up a wall." But the third man said enthusiastically and with pride, "I'm building a cathedral." No doubt, the third bricklayer was bound for success.

Once you have created an excellent culture and work environment, the flip side of that coin is to have high-performance expectations. The creation process can be sequential or in parallel, but long term one thing is true and constant: your culture and environment will drive performance.

LEADERSHIP LESSON

Life is too precious and too short to be squandered in mediocrity. Pursue something that sets you on fire and become the best possible version of you. Burn so brightly that you cause those around you to reassess their commitment to excellence.

Freedom in Ownership

Several years ago, a nurse sent me an email in the middle of the night. She was owning a mistake she had made. She had been administering medication to a patient. In the room next to her, she could hear a patient becoming volatile with a colleague. Physically, she was in one room administering medications, but mentally she was next door trying to support her colleague. In an effort to help her teammate, she rushed through a safety check in the process of giving the meds to her patient. And yet, her subconscious would not allow her to move forward. Just as the patient began taking the pills, the nurse quickly commanded, "Wait!" She then took the pills from the patient, conducted a proper safety check to ensure the medication was intended for this patient, and realized the medications were meant for another patient. She straightened things out with her patient and ultimately provided support to her coworker who was being berated by an unruly individual.

What she did next was incredibly impressive. She immediately sent our chief nursing officer and me an email detailing the mistake she had made. She took responsibility for her actions and even agreed to teach others the difficult lesson she learned that night.

I am a firm believer that no matter how good someone is at what they do, if they are in a hostile and disruptive environment, they will never be able to perform at their peak. Additionally, I could not have been more grateful for the email she sent. She could have easily swept the incident under the rug, and it likely would have never made it on anyone's radar. But because of the culture we had created where we receive feedback as a precious gift and lead change, she became an even greater leader in our organization. This type of event does not happen in an environment dominated by fear. But in the environment we had created, what this nurse did was welcomed and rewarded.

The thing about caregiving is that it is about life and death as well as about a lot of pain in between. This means no one, including you, would want to go to an average hospital. Regardless of our role or industry, we should constantly be pursuing higher standards to improve the world around us, with the ultimate goal of setting *the* standard.

What Are You Willing to Accept?

Adopting this mentality at the first hospital where I served as president, we began to see strong improvements. It was not uncommon for our facility to be the leader in certain metrics across a world-renowned healthcare system. As we would hit these milestones, you could sense the organizational sigh of relief. We had finally arrived at our destination. As this happened, we deployed the following philosophy: If a metric is worth our time to track, we want to be the best in the healthcare system or in the top decile nationally. Were we always there? No, but we were always striving to be there.

One day I was speaking with one of our directors of nursing regarding our performance on a stroke protocol. The key initial metric when caring for a stroke victim is referred to as "door to needle time." This time starts the moment the patient crosses the threshold of our facility until the time we begin deploying a clot-busting agent to restore blood flow, assuming the patient is a candidate for it. Why is this door to needle time so important? For every minute that passes when someone is having a stroke, two million brain cells die. Good care versus great care can literally mean the difference between a stroke victim walking out of the hospital a couple of days later or spending the rest of their life with some sort of deficit or worse. At our facility, our time in this metric was good but not great.

As I was asking questions about our process and if we were parallel processing tasks whenever possible, the nursing director interrupted me and said, "I know. You want us to be perfect." I responded, "I don't expect us to be perfect . . . but pretty close." With that in mind, our team set out to develop the most efficient and effective process possible.

A few months after several improvement iterations, I ran into the spouse of one of our stroke patients. Her husband had arrived at our hospital with paralysis on most of the left side of his body, slurred speech, and a general inability to communicate. He received the medication through a much-improved process. This grateful wife went on to share how her husband was about to be discharged to go home and without any lingering symptoms. In two days he had gone from a life-threatening situation to going home with zero deficits. The elation and gratitude expressed by his wife was worth more than any trophy we could ever receive. We shared this story throughout the facility to reiterate the importance of what we do and why it is vitally important that we be great at what we do.

Embrace Your Ignorance

At one point, after receiving a promotional opportunity, I spent the first couple of months in the new role doing the "new guy" thing—asking a lot of questions and trying to learn the organization. Assuming you are not boarding a sinking ship and need to take immediate actions, this initial approach is important for several reasons:

1. It conveys respect for the people and work that has been done prior to your arrival. People are much more likely to be accepting of new ideas if they feel appreciated and heard. This only happens if you have invested the appropriate amount of time to learn about the existing team and processes.
2. It allows you to learn more about how and why people do what they do. As seasoned as we may be, we should always be in learning mode. When we assume we know

all we need to know, we inadvertently create personal blinders. Additionally, if we foster the perception that we do not need information, we will impede organizational transparency.

3. It creates a mutually dependent environment which fosters relationship building. The expression "Teamwork makes the dream work" is predicated upon relationships. Without strong relationships, there will be no team, no meaningful work, and certainly no realization of a dream.
4. It provides an opportunity for you to craft a personalized approach to your relationships, work, and leadership rather than pulling out your favorite cookie cutter. Walking into a new organization, we should never assume anything. If you have seen one organization, do not assume you have seen them all. Former strategies may or may not be applicable in the new environment. As a side note, make it a point to never reference your previous organization with the implication that the new organization should emulate the old one. It annoys people. If you do reference your previous organization, mind your pronouns. Your new organization demands "we"; your former organization became "they" the moment you left it and joined the new one. The sooner you flip your mindset, the quicker you will begin building your team.
5. It demonstrates the process of receiving feedback as a gift. Great leadership requires a high level of listening and reflection. That does not mean everything should be done at a snail's pace. On the contrary, it simply calls on us to listen as often as possible, which inevitably creates

a relationship-oriented culture where people are truly valued rather than a transactional environment where people are viewed similar to tangible assets.

As I would sit in meetings and review innumerable trend charts denoting our performance on a myriad of metrics, one thing became clear: we did not employ benchmarks or external comparisons. Routinely, presenters would talk about the trend line in absence of any reference point other than our own facility target.

After a few of these meetings, I began to ask the new-guy question, "What is the benchmark for this metric?"

The consistent response from the subject matter experts was, "Well, the health system average is X," or "The national average is Y."

I would then ask, "What is the best performance in the system, or what is the top decile performance nationally?" and follow it by, "We will never aspire to average!" In some cases, we may have to work to get to average, but that will only be a milestone in the process to being the best we can be. It was a rarity for anyone in the room to be able to answer either question related to best-in-class benchmarking.

Too often we get comfortable with our own organizational goal. After all, if we hit our local target, we get a good review and hopefully a nice merit increase at the end of the year. Instead, I urge that you forget about your annual performance review and merit increase when setting goals. Those are just by-products of creating your best every day. Your best must always be your focus.

To shift our mindset, we began plotting our actual performance, our facility target, and either the best performance in the system or the top decile in the nation. This is something we had done a few years earlier at the first hospital. There were the usual comments along the lines of "That might be demoralizing to the team." My response? Forget about demoralizing ourselves! Focus instead on demonstrating love for our patients and taking pride in what we do. Other comments turned out to be rooted in embarrassment and avoidance because we were so far off of any acceptable benchmark that we did not want to look in the mirror and face reality. We had several conversations about pursuing our potential versus being dumbed down by a local target.

Someone somewhere must be the best. Why not us? Why not you or your team or your organization?

By reframing our reference point, we routinely began to surpass our facility target in pursuit of something much loftier—excellence. At the end of the day, I would much rather pursue the setting of a higher standard and fail than to pursue an easily attainable local goal and succeed.

LEADERSHIP LESSON

The greater danger for most of us lies not in setting our aim too high and falling short; but in setting our aim too low, and achieving our mark.
—Michelangelo

Never fear the pursuit of excellence! Embrace it. Allow the tension between excellence and reality to be your fuel each day.

Six-Tenths of a Second

On May 6, 1954, Roger Bannister broke the previously unbreakable four-minute-mile barrier, with a time of three minutes, fifty-nine and four-tenths of a second. World-class runners had been chasing this goal for decades without success. Prior to Bannister's accomplishment, many top minds of the time believed a sub four-minute mile to be a physical impossibility.

Bannister took a methodical approach to training that he developed himself. Before he broke the record, many experts criticized his approach, with some speculating that it would take pristine conditions, no wind, no rain, a mild temperature, and a hard surface even assuming it possible for someone to break the four-minute barrier. Yet, on a cold and windy day, on a wet track at Iffley Road Track in Oxford, England, Bannister beat the barrier when experts thought it could not be done.

Six-tenths of a second changed everyone's mindset. Six-tenths of a second liberated countless athletes and coaches. Forty-six days after Bannister's accomplishment, an Australian runner, John Landy, also broke the barrier. Within a year, two more runners were below four minutes *in the same race*. Since Bannister, more than one thousand four hundred men have broken the four-minute mile. It is now considered the standard for professional distance runners.

That Is Unrealistic

On a local level, with far less notoriety than Roger Bannister but still important to our patients, was a conversation one team had about our inpatient room cleaning process. With the growth we experienced, we needed beds to be cleaned quickly so we could admit patients in a timely manner who were awaiting a bed. Technically speaking, there are twenty-eight minutes of work that must be accomplished when terminally cleaning a room between patients. This is something we cannot slack on.

As Jim, the regional director for Environmental Services, and I were discussing our opportunities one day, I suggested a target that encompassed from the moment we knew we needed a room to the point that the room was actually ready to be occupied. The target time was thirty-five minutes—a goal we had occasionally achieved under ideal circumstances. The math was simple. We would have seven minutes to respond to a vacant room and begin the cleaning process, with the rest of the time dedicated to finishing the cleaning work. When I suggested setting a thirty-five-minute standard, Jim's response was, "Well, that's just unrealistic."

I interrupted him and said, "If we start with the mindset that it's unrealistic, it will be! Our challenge as leaders is to figure out how we make it a reality. If we believe we can't, we won't. Leadership is about making it happen, not accepting it won't happen."

We left the meeting with an agreement that we would give our best effort to figure out how we get to thirty-five minutes. Through several process design efforts, we went on to routinely hit that target. This meant we consistently got our patients into a more comfortable setting faster than other facilities who were fine waiting two to four times longer for a room to be terminally cleaned. That may not seem like a big deal, but over the course of a year we eliminated thousands of hours of wait time for our patients and were able to initiate their care plans sooner. This translated into better care simply because we did a better job of cleaning vacant rooms. Our hospital became the system's benchmark for room turnovers.

As theoretical physicist Albert Einstein said, "We can't solve problems by using the same kind of thinking we used to create them." Too often, we allow our life experiences to artificially, and sometimes unconsciously, set limits on our aspirations. Instead, allow yourself to dream. While you are at it, you might as well dream big and be willing to do the work to make your dream a reality.

3

THIS PLACE IS DIFFERENT

When you can do the common things of life
in an uncommon way, you will command
the attention of the world.
—George Washington Carver

Our first hospital saw tremendous improvement in team member engagement, quality outcomes, customer satisfaction, growth, and financial performance because of the culture our team built. Our team's care and outcomes were recognized with numerous honors and ultimately national recognition. Subsequently, I was offered an opportunity within our organization to do something similar at a larger facility. Our second hospital, even more impressively experienced tremendous improvement in outcomes because of the culture our team built. This time we did it in a shorter time frame and in a highly competitive and mature market.

The first hospital was in a rural suburb setting. By all rights, it was a well-run facility, but the physical plant had been held together by duct tape and chewing gum and needed to be replaced. Thankfully, a replacement facility was underway when I arrived. It was a hectic time, and I loved it. We began our cultural transformation at the old facility six months before moving into the new one.

The day of the move from the old to the new plant went incredibly smoothly. Anticipating the public excitement around the new facility, we routinely discussed the fact that people are going to come kick the tires because we have a shiny new building. The only way they would come back and, more importantly, go home and tell their family and neighbors about us was if they received a world-class experience and care. We held several leadership think-tank sessions to discuss the needs of our growing organization. Although we had moved to a new location, many members of our team retained the "hunker down and try to survive" mentality required at the old facility.

Mindset Is Everything

We metaphorically discussed how we had been handed the keys to a brand new battleship, and we needed to be on the offensive. To exemplify this mental shift, one day a leader boastfully shared with me how a physician wanted to start offering a new procedure that would require a capital investment. It was a higher acuity procedure that historically was not performed at the old hospital. She proudly proclaimed, "I told the physician, 'We don't do that stuff here.'"

I paused for a moment as she basked in the glow of her proclamation and replied, "Yet! We don't do that *yet*. Our job is to figure out how we make it happen."

Within a couple of months, we were offering the new procedure to our patients. No longer did patients have to travel twenty minutes to a larger facility to benefit from the procedure. They could now stay in their own community and receive exemplary care. It was an important lesson on how we needed to transform our mindset to coincide with our new facility. We should have been asking, "How can we better serve our community?" rather than hanging on to dogma that would have mentally imprisoned us in the old facility.

Let the Fun Begin

For our first year in the replacement facility, we were budgeted to lose over eleven million dollars due to an expected slow growth rate and tremendous depreciation on the new plant. Instead of losing millions of dollars, we miraculously made twenty-six thousand. More importantly, our team member engagement, quality outcomes, and patient experience scores improved substantially by consistently applying the process of loving, listening, and leading.

To honor this Herculean effort, we held a food truck celebration for our team on multiple shifts and multiple days. While most hospitals are not excited about an operating margin below 1 percent, we were! I informed my boss, "I believe we can say we are the only hospital in the United States who spent their entire bottom line on an around-the-clock food truck celebration for their team!" The food trucks that year cost twenty-four thousand dollars. This was a simple gesture, but more importantly it was an expression of gratitude and care for the people who created these great outcomes. This was a Camelot-like time in our history, but our focus remained on creating a loving environment.

Whether we are greeting someone with a smile or working on a new service offering, we should always do so with a mindset of excellence. In the healthcare industry, people typically do not go to the hospital for a fun event. Usually a negative concern in their life has brought them to our door. They often come to us filled with fear and anxiety. Our opportunity with each patient is to replace their fear and anxiety with love and compassion while delivering impeccable care. This happens through our interactions with one another. Again, it is the difference between someone receiving care and actually feeling cared for. Everyone is going to have a different lens on this as well. A nurse, a doctor, and an administrator all bring differing abilities to bear. Each must play their part in the orchestra of teamwork to achieve top-notch outcomes.

We must figure out in every unique interaction, "How can I provide the care this person needs in a loving manner so they also feel cared *for*?" We lightly remind one another that the only time when someone might come to the hospital for a fun reason is to have a baby. Even with that life-changing experience, mom and dad are going to have different definitions of what fun looks like. Regardless of your role or industry for that matter, figuring out how to provide your service in a loving manner will allow you to consistently exceed expectations.

At the first hospital, it became a common occurrence for someone to visit it and make the following comment: "You can feel there is a difference here when you walk in." One day a visiting executive walked into our administrative suite and facetiously commented, "From being greeted at the information desk to walking down the hallway, it was really weird. Everyone I met smiled and said hello!" We will take that kind of weird. Everyone smiling and greeting passers-by in the hallways of our organization were simply by-products of our organization's cultural expectations. The warmth of a smile is not a job requirement, but it certainly does make a difference in attitudes and experiences.

After hearing a number of people talk about how our organization was different in a good way, we began asking them to define what they meant by "different" in an attempt to codify what was resonating with team members and visitors. We were hoping to distill the feedback into some type of top ten list. The feedback turned into a top eighty-seven list! We spent several days reviewing the information to determine what mattered the most to our organization. As I sat reviewing and considering all the amazing feedback and traits that had been listed to describe our difference, three trends emerged, which we turned into principles.

Three Principles

The first trend was the timeless yet simple philosophy of *love one another*, or as I like to say, "Love one another but always in an HR appropriate manner!" Using the term *love* in a business setting can easily make people feel uncomfortable. For any organization to talk about creating a loving environment, there is a great deal to unpack in order to operationalize this concept. I will discuss this much more extensively in the ensuing pages.

The second concept that came from the trends was to *welcome feedback.* When I say welcome feedback, I am not just talking about being willing to listen to criticism. You must view feedback as a precious gift. Most people love to receive encouraging feedback, such as "You did a great job on that presentation" or "I am really impressed with your work ethic." Far too often, however, we are much less enthusiastic about receiving feedback if the comments are critical. No one likes to hear, "The baby is ugly!"

I remember when our son was born. I thought he was the most beautiful child in the history of humanity. As amazing an infant as he was, there were occasions where he would spit up, needed his diaper changed, or needed a haircut. The biggest challenge in welcoming feedback as a precious gift is our ego or a preconceived notion of reality. If we are willing to check our egos and, as leadership expert Stephen Covey would say, "Listen to understand rather than to respond," we can gain so much more out of the wealth of feedback around us. The other concern with dismissing feedback is that if you are unwilling to listen, it will not be long before the people around you have nothing to say. As you might anticipate, this is a terrible place to be.

The third concept we instilled in our culture, no matter what heights we may have achieved, was to *constantly lead change*, especially when receiving feedback. How many times have you heard the phrase that people "naturally resist change"? What we found is that people resist loss, not necessarily change. A beautiful quote about change and loss came from the Italian philosopher Niccolò Machiavelli when he said, "Nothing is more difficult to take in hand, more perilous to conduct, or more uncertain in its success, than to take the lead in the introduction of a new order of things." Most people are actively invested in whatever structure renders their regular paycheck, sustains their livelihood, supports their family, or allows them to plan for their future. All these items are things most of us would fight for with all our might. If people appreciate why we must change and what the upside looks like, they are much more likely not only to support it but also and more importantly to promote it. And that is part of the secret sauce of leadership.

The Navy Seals, arguably the most elite fighting force on the planet, have a mantra of getting 1 percent better every day. As they set the standard for military forces, they still desire to improve daily. Why would we not want to do the same thing for our customers? It is an age-old challenge because success can breed contentment and complacency. We routinely utter the saying that we never want to break our own arm patting ourselves on the back. If we are good at something, we aspire to be great. If we are great at something, we aspire to set the standard. This is a never-ending iterative process of climbing to new heights regardless of what we have already accomplished. The challenge is to always celebrate milestone achievements without being satisfied with how far you have come. Part of our culture is reminding ourselves that someone must be the best at delivering care, so why not us? Why not *you*? That question is not posed in an arrogant manner but as a means for continually challenging ourselves. If we genuinely love our team, our patients, and the communities we serve, why wouldn't we want the best for them? Why would we not strive to provide the best we can humanly offer?

Leaders sometimes refer to this approach as "that love stuff." Make no mistake about it, this is not about holding hands around the campfire and singing kumbaya, although there is nothing wrong with that. Nonetheless, if we express love as our primary aspiration, we should be compelled to deliver the highest standards possible. We should never settle for okay or even good. We should constantly be striving for better. *Love never settles. It inspires and it grows.* Could you imagine running an advertising campaign with the slogan, "Come to our hospital (or business). We are okay." Absolutely not! So why allow mediocrity to live in your organization? It occurs everywhere, every day—in our organization and in yours. Our opportunity is to create an environment where *unexceptional* behavior and outcomes stick out like a sore thumb, where there's an environment that views *mediocrity* as offensive. Through finding love in our work and loving the process, we will inherently achieve greater and greater heights—the genuine by-products of love as a strategy.

LEADERSHIP LESSON

Know your personal and organizational values. Be certain everyone in the organization knows them and that everyone is living those values daily as if your next breath depended on it. Get a diverse group of people together, influencers who can help lead the cause, and define that for which you want to be known culturally. Next, operationally define excellence. Then determine where your biggest gaps exist between current reality and where you want to be and get after filling in the gaps.

I once heard a CEO describe this process as follows: "We are on a difficult journey. We will carry the wounded, and we will shoot the stragglers." Certainly not the most loving imagery, but the message about closing the gap was crystal clear.

As you move through this process, one thing is certain: if hypocrisy is the disease, consistency is the cure. Recommit each day to pursuing the highest standards possible, even if you are immediately shooting for a specific milestone along the way.

4
LOVE OF CULTURE

Culture eats strategy for breakfast.
—Peter Drucker

These three tenets,

1) Love one another
2) Welcome feedback as a precious gift
3) Lead continuous change

have become the foundation for cultural excellence at two different award-winning hospitals.

The quote above by Peter Drucker is so true. When mentoring leadership teams over the years, I have added to the phrase, "If we are excellent at culture *and* strategy, we get to eat whatever we want!" A strong culture is no excuse to sleep on strategy. To the contrary, a great culture will allow you to achieve greater execution related to strategy.

A maxim that we routinely share is that the only acceptable outcome of our actions and efforts is excellence. This philosophy is lived out through our relationships with one another and to the organization. These relationships contain the transformative energy that guides our organization and defines our culture.

Many leaders view culture as "soft stuff" and prematurely dismiss intentional cultural work, opting instead for the more tangible initiatives that lend themselves to financial equations. In the words of Julia Roberts's character in *Pretty Woman*, "Big mistake! Big! Huge!" Often leaders seem to fear cultural work because they struggle to define it. Here's how I see it: *Culture is that powerful intersection between what we say we value as a collective group and how we actually behave*. Unfortunately, this powerful intersection is too often underleveraged. What I've found is that the greater the alignment of these two factors, the greater the cultural impact. As referenced above, a strong culture allows for better execution of strategic plans and operational tactics. Instead of employees showing up to exchange labor for wages and perform the minimal amount of work required to satisfy their job description, you end up with team members working together to care for one another and ultimately your customers. Job descriptions become a baseline standard or a starting point for expectations rather than all that's required. Ultimately, *excellence is the expectation and only acceptable outcome*.

For practical application, let us look at culture and values in the four-box approach:

Figure 1

Here is a description of what life is like in organizations represented by each quadrant:

- In the lower left-hand corner, *weak values and weak behaviors* create a dumpster fire. No one stays at these organizations. (We will explore experiences with a couple of dumpster fires later.)
- In the upper left-hand box, *strong values and weak behaviors* create a culture of hypocrisy. This type of organization has minimal lasting impact. They may have their values and mission statement framed nicely on a wall, but their actions seldom reflect their values.
- The lower right-hand box represents organizations with *weak values and strong behaviors*. They are typically the result of leadership not clearly defining what is important, but despite executive leadership, a few good people in the organization may actually be some-

what productive. The environment is the result of a leadership vacuum, creating serious cracks in internal relationships and productivity. Sure, some things may still grow despite the cracks, which may lead some leaders to think like Jim Cary's character in the movie *Dumb and Dumber* did: "So you're telling me there's a chance!" A chance for good to occur, yes, but not because of strong values linked with consistent and solid behaviors from leadership.
- Finally, the remaining box represents organizations with *strong values and correspondingly strong behaviors*. This is the ultimate goal for which all of us should strive. It's like the late 1970s television show *Fantasy Island*. If you recall the reference, those guests who went to Fantasy Island to have a dream come true did not always experience rainbows and bunny rabbits. They learned some tough life lessons and, in the process, left the island better people due to the improved alignment with their values and behaviors. (As a child, I dreamt of being Mr. Roarke, the island's mysterious and wise overseer, but the closest I have come is having premature gray hair.)

Like it or not, every organization will have a culture. Great organizations plan for and ensure behavioral alignment related to the type of culture they desire. Nothing is left to chance. Generating this alignment represents the foundation of what leaders should be focused on daily and over the long-haul. This is the work that ultimately creates a "different" environment.

LEADERSHIP LESSON

Never leave the most foundational element of your organization to chance. Define the type of culture you desire and check every decision against that definition. At some point, the decision-making process will become subconscious in relation to your culture. Every person on the team will own the culture and outcomes. Deviations from excellence will be checked and corrected at the interaction point between your team and consumers.

Signs of Love

Now, back to that love-one-another principle for just a moment. This simple concept should cover everything we do in life. Love is arguably the most powerful force in the universe. From a relationship standpoint, the connection between love and success is obvious. Love in a leadership or business arena is about caring for your customers and the people who create value for your customers. It is about caring for the process of leadership that hopefully creates value for the people who touch your customers. And yet, when I throw the "L" word into a business or leadership forum, I find many people instantaneously becoming uncomfortable. But why? After all, I'm not talking Chuck Woolery and the Love Connection, or, for a more contemporary reference, Tinder.

Early in my career I read a quote by the CEO of a well-known pizza company. He said, "If you don't make it, bake it, or take it you better be supporting those who do." As a leader and a non-clinician working in the healthcare industry, that statement resonated to my marrow. In our onboarding orientation for new team members, I routinely share, "I have minimal clinical skills. If you ever see me rendering care, *please* intercede on behalf of the patient! That said, a *huge* part of my role is to care for the people who care for the people." If I pursue excellence in caring for our team, they will inherently be equipped to provide excellent care to the communities we serve. The servant-oriented nature of the pizza example creates a higher calling than doing the minimum expected for the given role. If we can approach every situation with that loving, servant orientation in mind, it opens so many avenues for us to lead. Our options become boundless, only limited by our own imagination.

Finally, if I tell my wife that I love her but forget her birthday or, in our tradition, "birthday month," or if I forget our anniversary, or if I fail to open doors and live out other gestures that convey love, she is likely to question my proclamation of love for her. On the other hand, if we truly love something or someone, our actions will support our words. We may have momentary lapses given our fallible humanness, but overall, there will be no doubt about how we feel about another person if we love them. And love absolutely demands excellence!

LEADERSHIP LESSON

Consider ancient cultures for a moment. We learn about them through cultural artifacts. If someone unfamiliar with your organization were to come in and study one of the modern-day artifacts of your culture there, what would they find? Make a list using the following chart to get you started.

Actual Findings	Preferred Findings
Busy meeting schedules	Leaders engaged in caring for their teams
Preference toward financial metrics	Preference toward people metrics
Focus on reports	Focus on stories
Culture dominated by fear	Culture dominated by love

Now compare your list to what you hope others would discover. The delta between those two points should leave you excited to get out of bed every morning and start working! Much like the Chinese proverb "The journey of a thousand miles begins with one step," this is not an overnight process. That said, moving the dial just a little each day creates an enormous improvement over time. In a year or two, you will look back at your organization, including the people and the outcomes, and you will be amazed at the extraordinary transformation that has taken place.

A Simple Message

A cultural artifact you will find in the two hospitals where I served as president is a simple bracelet with a powerful message. One day I received an email from a young man who worked in our Emergency Department, Dustin Hatley. In the email, he shared how he wears a rubber bracelet that serves as a reminder of the comforting message, "God Is Big Enough." Witnessing difficult life situations on a daily basis in the Emergency Department, Dustin took the initiative to offer a bracelet to patients and family members who might need some encouragement. In the email, Dustin expressed how he was hopeful that his practice was acceptable and wanted to know if the hospital would be willing to buy the next bag of one hundred bracelets as he had paid for the first bag. My response was a resounding yes! I was so impressed with his initiative and display of love and compassion for people in their time of need.

As we met to discuss how we might further his idea, he shared with me how he went through some difficult times as a young, single father. While facing his challenges, someone gave him one of the bracelets to serve as a constant reminder that everything was going to be alright. Dustin, knowing pain and grief himself, wanted to help others bear the pain and grief that landed them in the hospital. After all, no one plans a trip to the Emergency Department.

As we discussed the idea, we put together an implementation plan that oddly enough was initially thwarted by one of our chaplains. He felt the bracelets were a gimmick. Nonetheless, we bought one thousand bracelets and even placed our logo on them. We gave them to team members, patients, family members . . . really anyone who wanted one. In no time at all, we had given all one thousand away and were reordering more.

To his credit, our chaplain shared the story of a family friend he ran into at a local grocery store who was wearing one of Dustin's bracelets. The lady's husband had recently been in the hospital and unfortunately passed away. As our chaplain was consoling the widow, she shared how much that little bracelet had served as a comforting reminder during her most recent few weeks of making difficult decisions and adjusting to her new life as a widow. Such a simple gesture had a powerful impact.

At the time of this writing, we have given out over one hundred thousand bracelets in the communities we serve. That is one hundred thousand sources of encouragement thanks to Dustin living out love for others. What a great cultural artifact!

LEADERSHIP LESSON

Simple ideas are sometimes the best ideas. Encourage people to consider new and improved ways of living out your organizational values. Promote them throughout the company whenever possible. To use a baseball metaphor, there will be an overwhelming number of singles, some doubles, fewer triples, and the occasional homerun. Celebrate them all. They give life to your team, to your organization, and ultimately to your customers.

5

BURN THE SHIPS

There is a difference between interest and commitment.
When you are interested in doing something,
you do it only when circumstances permit.
When you are committed to doing something,
you accept no excuses, only results.
—Art Turock

Have you ever made a New Year's resolution and kept it? I am not a fan of waiting until January 1 to commit to doing something I already know needs to be done. If you need to make a change, simply determine your plan of action and get after it. Do not wait for some magical date on a calendar. Be action-oriented in all phases of your life.

Studies show that only 8 percent of all New Year's resolutions are kept all year long. Roughly 80 percent of resolutions are abandoned by February. Having worked out in many gyms over the years, there is always the comical influx of well-intentioned people during January and maybe February. But most of them don't show up the other ten months of the year. There are a variety of reasons why 92 percent of New Year's resolutions fail, but ultimately those reasons lead back to that pesky "C" word—commitment.

In 334 BC, Alexander the Great led a fleet of ships across the Dardanelles Straits to conquer Darius III and the Persian Empire. At the time, the Persian Empire was the largest empire the world had ever known. Upon landing in what is now modern-day Turkey and despite being vastly outnumbered by the seemingly endless Persian army, Alexander ordered his men to burn their ships.

Stop for just a moment and ponder how those soldiers might have felt about the order to abandon their only option for retreat should the vast Persian army overwhelm them. One could imagine responses all over the spectrum from "Let's do this" to "Wait, what?" to "Alex has lost it!" As legend has it, Alexander's leaders begged him to reconsider this questionable command. In a defining moment, Alexander told his men, "We will either return home in Persian ships, or we will die here!" Talk about motivation to stick with your resolution!

A slightly more popular version of this symbolic act occurred more than one thousand years later when the Spanish conquistador Hernán Cortez landed in modern-day Mexico. Concerned about defections and to eliminate any possibility of retreat, Cortez scuttled his own ships in a commitment to conquer or die in the attempt.

Both examples are pivotal moments used to galvanize a group of people into a singular mindset: conquer or die trying; there's no middle ground. That is the type of mindset that consistently leads to success. Even in the face of losses, when dealing with extreme difficulties, successful leaders and successful teams lock in mentally and emotionally on their goal. Could either of those military efforts have failed? Certainly, but the commitment required to destroy their route of escape carried both armies to uncommon commitment and ultimately to victory.

At both hospitals where I have served as president, we had more than our fair share of challenges. We certainly had setbacks on our path to excellence. Nonetheless, with each setback, we welcomed feedback and began to lead in another direction. A team leader once described our process and commitment as an eighteen-wheeler carrying a huge load up a hill. At certain junctures you simply must gear down to continue making progress, even if it is at a decreased rate. Eventually, though, you regain momentum and speed to propel yourself along the journey—until you hit the next great hill to climb. The key to maintaining commitment to excellence is to eliminate alternatives to excellence. Unfortunately, those options come in all shapes and sizes and can be extremely enticing.

Let's Eat

The second hospital served a very affluent community. For years, this hospital's market was known as "the land of milk and honey," denoting the favorable market conditions. Over the years, competitors, hoping for a piece of the pie, flooded this market and made it increasingly difficult to generate margins previously experienced by our hospital.

In year one, we saw nice year-over-year growth because of our focus on culture and deployment of key strategies. Year two, we were faced with an ever-increasing financial target of historic proportions. Our senior leadership team at times seemed paralyzed by the aggressive goal. I shared with them in one particularly contentious meeting, "We need to stop wringing our hands over how to make X and place our energy on figuring out how we make 2X!" That statement was met with a mixture of raised and furrowed brows, but it also changed our mindset from fretting about our current target to thinking about a much bigger future. Additionally, it helped reframe the current challenge as a milestone on our way to that brighter future. Please know, our focus was never on becoming more profitable, something all hospitals struggle with, but on driving a loving culture. In the interest of sustainability that must be the goal.

One great way to maintain commitment and momentum is to simply avoid distractions. Every person and organization will routinely have options to consider. Knowing when to say no is just as important as knowing and remembering that to which you are committed. Out of concern, our team was becoming distracted by what seemed to be unfair, unrealistic, or too aggressive. We dealt with this by focusing on a much larger goal over a longer time frame. That helped us to galvanize our attention, and we achieved the overly aggressive goal in a shorter time period. Committed human beings never cease to amaze me with what they can accomplish absent distractions.

On a personal level, my wife and I had a pastor early in our marriage who, while speaking to a large group about marital commitment, instructed, "Whenever someone begins to flirt with you, as enticing as it may be, immediately bring your spouse up in the conversation." We all need a daily reminder of why we are committed to our commitments. Without reminders and boundaries, our attention wanes, we lose focus, and before you know it, we are overwhelmed with mediocrity and disappointment. This concept is similar to the parable of boiling a frog. If you immediately place the frog in hot water, it will reject the environment and flee. If you introduce the frog to room temperature water, allow it to get comfortable while gradually increasing the heat, the frog will be finished before it knows what happened.

No Off-Ramp

Many people and businesses struggle because, on the road to excellence, they are willing to accept the off-ramp to comfortability. In addition to distractions, being comfortable is a great way to lose commitment to something that is going to challenge you and take you out of your comfort zone.

Years ago, I worked out at a CrossFit gym that had a phrase painted on the wall that read, "Embrace the suck." It is a simple phrase with a strong meaning. What we were going to experience in the gym for roughly an hour was going to be difficult, but it was also going to make us stronger. If we want to improve each day, we must do something we were not able to do yesterday or get better at something we were merely good at yesterday. Nothing worthwhile ever grows in a comfort zone, but it is oh so tempting to hang out in our comfort zone for just a little while. Pretty soon that "short break" turns into a year, then a decade, then a legacy.

Whether in your marriage, in your fitness, or in your business, if you will daily recommit to your goal, realize when to say no to things that may seem good but are ultimately goal killers, you will go so much further in life than if you take the routine pit stop in Mediocreville. Here are some simple steps that will, if followed, enable you to remain committed for a year or a lifetime:

1. Develop a goal that inspires the life inside of you—something that makes you a little uncomfortable.
2. Determine if others need to be involved. If so, cast the vision.
3. Break the big goal down into smaller goals.
4. Track and trend each of the goals and know how they support one another.
5. Continually reassess your progress and determine if you need to course correct in any areas.

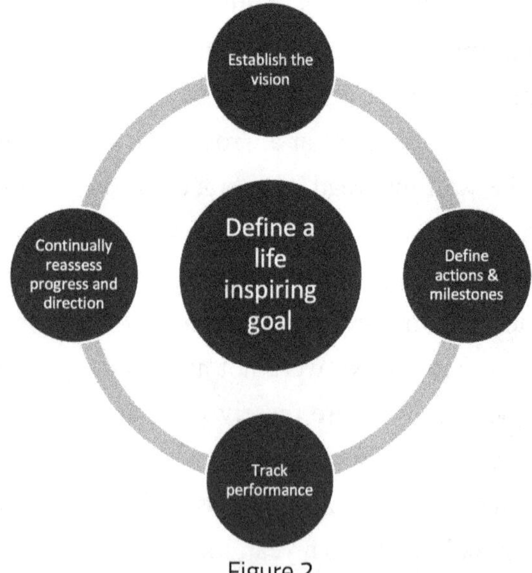

Figure 2

I personally used this process when I decided to write this book. As I told a colleague, if this sells two copies to my wife and me, or two hundred thousand, I am a better person for having gone through the process.

LEADERSHIP LESSON

Commitment to excellence should scare you just a little. What "ships" do you need to burn so that your team or organization can move on to set higher standards? If you want to live a life that impacts the world around you, reject comfort. Commit to something that inspires you, that breathes life into you. Once you determine what that is, you will become a roaring flame that will attract and inspire others.

Practically speaking, your entire organization must understand what you will accept and what you will reject. Certain people may choose to spend their energy protecting the "ships" versus pursuing the future. This simply cannot be tolerated. Cast a clear vision for where you are headed. Provide ample opportunity for clarity and alignment and get moving. Make no mistake about it, your "Darius" awaits. How committed are you and your team?

Know this, by February when resolve is starting to wane, some folks are going to start talking about building new ships to replace the old ones. In all your efforts and communications, remain focused on Darius.

6

LOVE REQUIRES HONESTY

Honesty is a very expensive gift.
Do not expect it from cheap people.
—Warren Buffett

First and foremost, we strive to create an environment where we prioritize and care for the people creating value for our customers. In our case, this means caring for the people who care for the patients. This is where extreme value and excellence are birthed. If people are properly cared for and understand the vision and their role in it, they will consistently outperform people who feel dismissed. A loving and trusting environment will consistently pave a pathway for people to be their best.

The Hay Group conducted a global study on employee engagement and found that engaged team members are 43 percent more productive than their disengaged counterparts.[2] It is important to note the practical difference between team members and employees. A team member is someone who has connected their personal purpose with the purpose of the organization; an employee is someone who shows up to collect a paycheck. We must strive for so much more than people showing up to exchange labor for wages. Obviously, everyone needs to be able to pay their bills, but in addition to creating a place where people can earn a living, we must create a place where people can live out their calling. For people to fully engage with an organization's mission, they must understand what role they play and that, on some level, someone at the organization cares for them. In an effort to move to a team-member mindset, have you ever asked someone:

1) What does demonstrating love to our customers mean to you?
2) How do you specifically demonstrate love to our customers?
3) How can our organization do a better job of demonstrating love for you?

This concept of caring for our teams has become lost in our society's fixation on short-term profit maximization. We constantly hear one generation complaining about the next, whether the topic is commitment, work ethic, or something else. A huge part of society's disengagement with employers is the lack of commitment companies have shown to workers. We have prioritized profits over people, forgetting that people create profits.

You Have Got to Be Kidding Me!

Earlier in my career, I accepted a position with another company that was offered under false pretense. My wife and I had resigned from our existing positions and sold our home, and we were two weeks out from the moving truck showing up to take us to the new city. We were excited until I received a call one afternoon. After exchanging greetings, the chief operating officer of the new company asked, "Are you sitting down?"

I replied, "That is a concerning way to start the conversation, but go ahead."

He went on to inform me that the position I had accepted would soon be eliminated, but new executive roles would be created, and they still felt I would be one of the more promotable leaders in the organization. They had been finalizing the new structure for months and still went forward with the search process for the role I had accepted. After explaining everything, they also offered a severance package if I wanted to walk away.

I have always abided by the philosophy, "It is far better to have a job when you are looking for one." With that, I told him, "Let me get my feet on the ground, show you what I can do, and we'll go from there." He seemed to be very appreciative of my response.

Soon after arriving at the new organization, I learned that they had planned on eliminating the position I accepted long before I had accepted it. They had not been truthful with themselves or with me. Two months later, internal politics between the chief executive officer and the chief operating officer led to the COO being let go. Personally, this created a very precarious situation since I was the new kid on the block and he was my primary connection to the organization. A couple of weeks later, my position was eliminated, and I transitioned from a corporate vice president to a facility chief operating officer.

Corporate leadership had previously informed me that the facility president with whom I was working had already been asked to look for a position outside of the organization due to poor performance and I would be in line for the vacated role. Certainly, a chaotic start, but it could not get worse, right?

Shortly after starting the newest role, I was serving as administrator-on-call for the system. The only call I received all week came on Friday evening. The nurse supervisor at our flagship facility called and frantically asked if I was available to come to the hospital. I replied, "Certainly. What's up?"

She stated, "We think [our chief executive officer] is in the emergency room!"

I thought that this guy was widely recognized throughout the state, so I asked her, "What do you mean you 'think' he is in the emergency room?"

She replied, "We have a motorcycle fatality without identification, and we believe it is [our chief executive officer]."

Within minutes I arrived at the hospital and tragically had to identify the body. I have never seen a human body in such a devastating condition. It was indeed our leader.

The next couple of weeks were a haze for everyone. As difficult as it was, in hindsight, it was probably a blessing in disguise that I was on call that week. Everyone else on the senior leadership team had served with our CEO for several years and had many memories of working with him. I was the newest member and was able to make the myriad of unsavory calls that evening to other leaders and board members.

After the grieving process began to subside, the claws came out! Here we were with our top two leaders gone in a matter of weeks. What took place next was nothing short of a political bloodbath. Everyone with any amount of political equity began jockeying for power. The chief human resource officer came to our facility to let me know that the board was extremely concerned with the amount of turnover and chaos in such a short period. Seeking to stabilize the organization, they chose to hire a professional coach to work with the facility president, to whom I now reported.

From Bad to Worse

The first couple of months of coaching were benign. Basically, the president and his coach met routinely to discuss his growth. At the two-month mark, the rest of our facility's senior team began meeting with the two of them. I will never forget the first session. We walked in the room to find Legos scattered all over the conference table. I thought, *Oh my gosh! We are living in a Dilbert cartoon!* Do not get me wrong. I loved Legos, but when I was a kid. Our assignment that day was to build something as individuals and tell the group what the object meant to us. I attempted something that hopefully resembled a tent because our family loved to go camping.

The following week brought more Legos. During this session, we had to build a structure and connect it to the person on either side of us. This was to reinforce our connectedness and interdependency.

Next came a group review of the wonderful book *Crucial Conversations*.[3] Unfortunately, the coach underestimated a couple of members on our team. Week one we were asked to share one strength each team member brought to the table. No problem. It was a nice and much needed uplifting moment. The following week, we had to offer one weakness each member brought to the team that could potentially derail the team. One key rule was that no one could pass on providing feedback to the other members.

To be respectful and to ensure no one was caught off guard by my comments, I met with everyone individually prior to our group session to share my feedback in a one-on-one setting. The conversations went very well. I am a big believer that for critical feedback to be optimized, it must be delivered with loving intentions. Additionally, whenever possible, we should offer praise in public and critique in private.

On the day of our critical feedback session, things were going fine until our chief financial officer provided our chief nursing officer with what seemed to be nebulous feedback. It did not go well. A couple of minutes into providing his feedback, our CNO went full DEFCON 1! The two of them engaged in a shouting match that quickly turned into a sobbing-uncontrollably shouting match! Both stormed out of the room unable to speak.

It was my turn to provide feedback. Five of us remained in the room and sat in silence for what seemed like an eternity awaiting our colleagues' return. I finally broke the silence by asking, "Can I go do some work?" Both the president and the coach requested everyone stay until the two who had left could regain their composure and rejoin the team.

After several more minutes, we were back together again. My turn at sharing feedback was anticipated to be much more relaxed since I had already had the conversations with each member of the team. All went well until I arrived at our CNO. As I began to share with her what I had shared a few days earlier, she began yelling at me and could not understand why I would say such things. I reminded her I had just shared the same feedback with her a few days ago in what seemed to be a very productive conversation. For the life of me, I still do not know why she became so volatile other than the fact that she allowed her emotions to overcome her.

Then we pressed on to our "hot button" conversation, an approach which is discussed in the book *Crucial Conversations*. Hot buttons are those topics or situations that could cause us to handle a situation poorly. As a prop, our coach provided each of us with a red glass bead about the size of a quarter. She instructed us to keep the bead in our pocket, and then told us that any time we were going to have a crucial conversation, we were to rub the bead in our pocket using our thumb and index finger. At that point, I had to remind our coach, with a little attempt at humor, that our industry is heavily dominated by women. Under no circumstances would I have a conversation with a lady while rubbing something in my pocket! Not happening. The next session, our coach brought clear glass beads for us to hold in our hands while conducting these difficult conversations. I appreciated the effort but felt quite comfortable having a serious conversation without the prop, not to mention how distracting it would be for both parties if one was rubbing a clear glass bead in plain sight while trying to conduct an important conversation.

Eventually I left this employer, the worst one I have ever had, and joined the best employer I have ever had.

Looking back on that situation, I wonder if the organization could have better sustained their leadership losses without spiraling downward so quickly if they had had a stronger culture.

LEADERSHIP LESSON

Companies love engaged team members. Sadly, too many leaders spend more time trying to figure out how to engage people than they do considering how engaged and committed they are to the people who come daily to create value for their customers. If more organizations flipped this equation and spent at least an equal amount of time on the latter, the former would become a nonissue. Like any good relationship, this all starts with honesty, transparency, and trust. Without these three, relationships are transactional in nature. With them in place, however, relationships are transformational.

What are you doing to cultivate honesty, transparency, and trust among your team?

What Is Good for the Goose . . .

Another company for whom I worked went through a restructuring process in the Corporate Human Resources department, effectively eliminating higher paying positions that would be backfilled with lower paying positions. This impacted the local business entities because the positions being eliminated lived and functioned in local entities. All the higher-level leaders whose jobs were being eliminated were good people who were in the wrong place at the wrong time.

As the backfill process ensued, one internal candidate was persistently negotiating her salary. The hiring corporate manager became offended that her initial offer was not joyfully accepted and exclaimed, "Where is the loyalty to the company!"

I told the hiring manager, "After what we just did to some great leaders, we do not get to sit on the throne of indignation and cast stones."

Where is the loyalty to the company? Probably the same place as the company's loyalty to the previously committed, high-performing team members who were just let go in favor of lower paid roles. And still, we wonder why many people in the workforce feel so little commitment to their employers.

We as employers need to initiate efforts to demonstrate commitment to our teams, unlike an executive I used to work with. Shortly after we began our working relationship, he came to me and said, "I think we can cut (a tenured director's) position."

I asked, "Is he performing poorly?"

"No," he replied.

I followed up with, "Have you asked him to do something he's been unwilling to do?"

"No. I just think we could cut the position."

This director had been with the organization more than two decades. Over the years, he had taken on multiple extracurricular assignments, worn different hats, and basically done anything that was asked of him, all with great outcomes. Striving to create a culture we could be proud of, I coached the executive, telling him that we would never be the organization we aspired to be if we went around handing out pink slips because we thought we could do without someone. Devaluing anyone devalues everyone. It leads to an environment in which people become fearful. In an organization motivated by love, on the other hand, living in fear is just not an option.

LEADERSHIP LESSON

Ancient Greek philosopher Aristotle said, "We are what we repeatedly do. Excellence, then, is not an act, but a habit." If we expect excellence, we must first create an excellent environment where excellence can reproduce. There is a reason farmers plant crops in fertile soil instead of on rocks. In the absence of honesty and transparency, you will be able to accomplish extraordinarily little in the way of positive organizational culture. This will inherently lead to mediocrity—or worse.

Ask yourself, *What grows best in our organization—love or fear?* After you answer the question, write down what grows best and then determine the best and most expeditious path to regaining the high ground through honesty, transparency, and trust. Routinely, leaders believe only they can bear the truth about their organization. My experience has been that frontline team members not only handle the truth but greatly aide in navigating forward.

We miss tremendous opportunities to tap into organizational wisdom when we withhold information by devaluing people. Deliver the information, good or bad, in a loving manner and ask for feedback. You will likely be pleasantly surprised with what you receive by entrusting others with organizational ownership.

7 LEADERSHIP AND INTEGRITY

It is true that integrity alone will not make you a leader, but without it you will never be one.
—Zig Ziglar

As with any successful team or organization, the right leadership makes all the difference in moving the organization forward. John Maxwell famously said, "Everything rises and falls on leadership." It is difficult to find exceptions where that does not work out as true.

Active Retirement

At one point in my career, I was transitioning into a new role. During the transition process, a prominent member of the leadership team had effectively engaged in "active retirement." On my first day in the new role, this individual strolled into the office mid-morning. As she introduced herself, she promptly apologized for being late, which, as it turns out, was her routine. She also demonstrated a pattern of producing poor work product with material errors.

On my third day in the new role, I was informed that she was sleeping in a meeting. I initiated a loving conversation to ask if she was feeling well. She affirmed she was feeling great. I then informed her I was made aware she was sleeping in a meeting, which was another routine of hers. I encouraged her to stand up in the meeting if she was feeling drowsy. She expressed, "I thought about standing up, but I didn't want to be rude." I assured her standing up would be far less offensive than sleeping. To get us on the same page, I made certain she appreciated what a poor example that set for the rest of the organization. There was no rational way to demand excellence from the rest of the organization if we tolerated such behavior on the leadership team. She was in complete agreement.

Over the next few weeks, she was able to stay awake while at work, did a much better job of showing up on time, but continued to generate poor work product.

Over the preceding two years, this organization had experienced several layoffs and had struggled to perform financially. I could not help but think of the families that had been impacted through job eliminations and the wounds that could have been avoided had this executive been pursuing excellence every day. This performance and subsequent decisions also took a toll on the organization as people were living in fear that they might be next on the chopping block.

When we held a final separation meeting with this executive, she expressed that she had been thinking about getting out of her role for a while. In my mind I was thinking, *You took action on that thought quite some time ago!* Even in separation we had a loving and respectful conversation. She apologized for having let the situation get to that point.

As you might imagine, her leaving produced a sigh of relief and appreciation among the larger leadership team who had been observing her poor performance for quite some time. One person explicitly stated, "I guess we are finally getting serious now." Make no mistake about it, people scrutinize what you say versus how you behave. Any inconsistency in the two sends an incredibly loud message to the rest of the organization. Recall Figure 1, the four-box reference to the intersection of values and behaviors. The upper left-hand box illustrates *strong values and weak behaviors*, creating a culture of hypocrisy. Tolerating this executive's behavior did just that—allowed hypocrisy to fester and harm our organization's culture.

As you might imagine, being new to the organization, some of my superiors had concerns that I might have acted too hastily. Reasonable questions about a fair evaluation process were posed. My response was consistent. Our entire leadership team knows what a poor job this person had turned in for quite some time: not showing up for work, sleeping in meetings, and producing errors in reports. Everyone knew about the situation and, worse yet, that it had long been tolerated. In my response, I made it clear that we expect nothing short of excellence. If we tolerate this subpar performance, we cannot demand excellence of anyone and hope to retain a shred of integrity or credibility. Additionally, if we had failed to address this leader's performance, we would have publicly insulted everyone in our organization who shows up daily to deliver their best while cosigning poor performance and behavior.

LEADERSHIP LESSON

Putting off the difficult conversations will do nothing but harm the organization and its members and prevent everyone from consistently pursuing excellence. Thoughtfully engaging in these conversations in a compassionate manner is a requirement of loving leadership.

As it relates to these conversations, the following guidelines have been incredibly helpful throughout the years:

1. Check your emotions so you are better able to work toward resolution. It is fine to be passionate, but always do your best to maintain control of your emotions.
2. Clarify the issue from multiple points of view. Inventor and automobile magnate Henry Ford suggested, "Don't find fault, find a remedy." While there is likely fault, spend the majority of your time on the remedy.
3. Respectfully communicate through face-to-face interaction. Conflict resolution is seldom aided by

electronic communication where writers and readers lose much of their ability to communicate.

4. Be crystal clear about desired outcomes and timelines. If improvement is not apparent, be clear and concise about ramifications.

Organizational Terrorism

We have all encountered these individuals at some point in life. I'm talking about leaders who function as internal terrorists. For some reason, they view leadership as a throne on which to sit and rule their kingdom rather than viewing it as an opportunity to serve others. They use fear as a motivational stick to get their subjects to produce. They derive their perceived power through titular authority and wield it as a weapon.

Early in my career, I encountered two leaders who would fall into the organizational terrorist category. They operated in a symbiotic, codependent relationship. Their modus operandi was to use fear and intimidation to "motivate" their workers.

As part of my transition into the new role, I met individually with every member of the leadership team and asked two questions I routinely pose when taking on a new assignment:

- How would you describe the culture of this organization?
- If you were in my shoes, what would be your top one or two priorities over the next six months?

Roughly 40 percent of the leaders began their response with a statement along the lines of "I don't know how much longer I am going to be here, so I am just going to put this out there."

At that point, each would offer their experience of being terrorized by one or both previously mentioned leaders. There was a subgroup of leaders who had each circled a date on the calendar by which they would be gone! Incredibly disappointed, I went into a full-court press to re-recruit key leaders. I asked each one to hang on a little while longer with the following promise: we would sit down again in six months to see if the working environment had improved.

Over the next few months, I engaged in intensive coaching with the two problematic leaders, working on the premise that if you genuinely care, you will have the needed conversation. We began the coaching process by sharing the difficult feedback received during my orientation. As you might expect, neither executive aspired to the descriptions offered by other members of the leadership team regarding their leadership style. Nonetheless, they had created an environment of severe distrust throughout our organization.

As part of the coaching process, I encouraged each executive to take ownership of their behavior to rebuild a trusting relationship with the remainder of the team. I shared a personal example from a mistake I had made as a young executive.

Learn from My Mistake

Our organization was in negotiations to switch from one supplier to another in a key service line. I felt we had the support of the key stakeholders. As time went on, the incumbent vendor began a slander campaign with our stakeholders using me as the target. For me, the process became more about me beating the vendor than serving our stakeholders. That was a big mistake.

My boss called me in and shared a letter he had received from our key stakeholders voicing their message of "no confidence" in me. He then shared his personal lesson as a young executive. While leading an organization, he had failed to listen to and care for the employees at the facility to the point that they were proposing a vote to unionize. In complete humility, he invited everyone available to join a town-hall style meeting where he openly apologized for not listening better and not being the type of leader they deserved. He shared with me that the union vote never came to pass, and he went on to serve faithfully at the organization.

I shared with the executives how I had called a meeting with the individuals who signed the "no confidence" letter and a few other folks for good measure. I stood at the door and greeted everyone to offer my personal apology for serving myself rather than others. Once everyone had arrived, I offered one more public apology to the group and expressed the values of loving leadership to which I aspire. It turned out to be an incredibly cathartic process for all involved. Like my previous boss, I went on to successfully serve that organization several more years.

With this information in hand, I encouraged each of the current problem leaders to do something similar in their own way. The coaching for each was to rebuild a bridge of trust from the larger leadership group all the way to the frontline team. They realized that building trust with a group they had been beating on was going to be difficult. They knew they needed to be patient and humble, allowing the members of our team to cross that bridge of trust at their own pace. This situation was a perfect example of what military officer, senator, and statesman Lewis Cass said:

"People may doubt what you say, but they will believe what you do." It was going to take a tremendous amount of action for these "terrorist" leaders to earn back the trust of the organization.

One of the executives followed through on the coaching. She offered what I perceived to be a heartfelt apology, expressing ownership and contrition for her behavior. Unfortunately, her relationships within the organization were irreparably damaged. I checked in with several individuals asking their thoughts on her comments. To a person, their responses ran along the thread of "We will see; actions speak louder than words."

The other executive never made an effort to convey ownership of her responsibilities. Even in the face of overwhelming feedback, she was too proud to admit any mistakes or offer an apology. Never allow yourself to fall into this pit! If you make a mistake, own it! Grow from it! Never hide from it or ignore it. Sticking your head in the sand will never resolve the issue, especially when it comes to mending relationships.

Over time, to move the organization forward, we eventually had to part ways with both leaders. The leader who offered the heartfelt apology seemed to genuinely learn and grow from the experience. She went on to progressively larger roles elsewhere and performed quite well. The more obstinate leader moved forward as well but seemingly with more bitterness. Life is too short to allow pride to derail your leadership journey and the many relationships you will develop along the way.

Surprisingly and sadly, there were numerous reports of spontaneous celebrations throughout the organization when the announcement was communicated that these two leaders had moved on. Team members were reported to literally be dancing at their team huddles. One physician shared as he communicated the news to his partners that one of his colleagues actually wept over the end of a very frustrating existence and the joy of a better future without having to leave the organization. For me, this reaction was indeed surprising. I knew the situation was bad. I did not fully appreciate how bad it was.

Taking the Next Step

In any instance of a leadership transition, there is a window of opportunity for all parties to move forward in a productive manner. For the organization, you must recruit new leaders who are tenaciously focused on serving rather than being served. It has been my experience that when this happens, the organization's performance will immediately take off. If handled appropriately, the intended improvements on the back end of the transition can yield exponential and sustainable improvement.

For the leader leaving the organization, it is common to experience the typical grief cycle. The sooner you get to the point of turning the corner from anger to acceptance, the better off you will be. A dear colleague went through such a transition with an abrupt departure. While it was a tough pill to swallow initially, it ended up being a great point of growth in his personal and professional life because of how he approached the situation.

LEADERSHIP LESSON

If you genuinely care about the people around you and the organization, you *will* lovingly engage in difficult conversations. Work to create a win-win situation for all involved.

You must also be able to realize when you are headed down a dead end and be willing to course correct. When the situation is headed toward the point of no return:

- Be as concise as possible in communicating expectations, timing, and repercussions. Prolonging the process will only prolong organizational agony.
- Be committed. When you say something, mean it. If milestones are not met, you cannot flinch on executing corrective actions, even if they require separation.

Any compromise in the process will almost certainly lead to failure.

8

CARING PRECEDES EXCELLENCE

People do not care how much you know,
until they know how much you care.
—US President Theodore Roosevelt

Early in her career, my wife, who happens to be a clinician, was caring for a baby who was born with a terminal condition. The baby was born with amniotic band syndrome—a condition in which bands develop from the inner lining of the amnion, the membrane that closely covers the embryo when first formed. These bands may attach to the infant and affect the development of different areas of the baby's body in utero. Tragically, the baby's brain and limbs were prevented from developing in utero. The parents were devastated. In their grief, they made many demands, one being a "brain transplant" for their child. When it was explained to them that the requested procedure had not yet been developed, the parents accused the care team of failing to provide all measures of care because they did not have the best medical insurance.

As my wife and two nurses attempted to pour out love and compassion onto these parents, their grief response was to threaten to murder my wife and the two nurses. For the next week, my wife and the nurses were escorted to and from the hospital by police officers. The hospital received multiple bomb threats as well. Concerned someone might show up at our home with ill intentions, we took our toddler forty-five minutes west of where we lived to spend a few days with my parents.

I grew up experiencing the outdoors and was extremely comfortable with firearms, but my wife was not. Reluctantly, she agreed to bring a handgun into our home for the first time in our marriage for personal protection. At the time, this was an angst-filled decision. Tensions were high, and the need for personal protection only made the tension greater. Now, after living in the great state of Texas for thirteen years, we own several guns. My wife even owns two of her own, and one is color coordinated with her car; apparently that is important.

Fortunately, these distraught parents never acted on their threats, but the situation they created was still a transformative experience for our family and for me professionally. It is difficult to imagine the anxiety created by such a threat until you are in the middle of the situation. Being a care provider is a physically and emotionally taxing role in someone's life. Mixing fear and intimidation into an already stressful situation should be unacceptable.

While this is obviously an incredibly egregious example of an unsafe work environment, abusive and caustic workplace behavior is rampant in our consumer-oriented society. One study by the American federal government's Occupational Safety and Health Administration found that healthcare workers were four times more likely than those in any other industry to be victims of workplace violence.[4]

When creating a safe environment, everyone in the organization must understand expectations around dignity and respect for all involved in the care process. You begin by communicating with your team how to treat one another. This should be built in part on formal organizational values. Before we will ever delight our customers, we must know how to care for our fellow team members. When behaviors deviate from expectations, just like anything else in life, if you expect excellence, there must be a remediation process.

By ensuring your team knows how to treat one another, the course correction discussion should be very straightforward. Once these expectations are clear and being lived out daily, treating customers in the same manner becomes an organic extension. The more challenging times come when a customer is treating your team poorly. This is no time to be timid. Any customer who abuses your team is not a customer you want. You are far better off to fire the customer than to allow your team to be abused. If you permit the abuse, you are inviting mediocrity into your organization.

LEADERSHIP LESSON

Before your team can fully care for your customers, they must feel cared for—fully. As a leader, this is one of the greatest gifts you will ever give to your team. This one element will transform your organization into a place where people can fully engage with their work. This type of environment will consistently lead to increasingly better outcomes in all facets of the organization.

Safety First

In my experience, employing the "nobody cares how much you know until they know how much you care" mantra drives team engagement. If every leader began their leadership practice with this philosophy, the world would be a much better place for workers and subsequently customers.

The cornerstone of demonstrating how much you care about your team is to refuse to allow them to be abused by customers. Set high standards for how you and others must treat your team. Permitting abusive behavior is a great demoralizing force in any industry. By permitting this type of behavior from customers or egotistical leaders, you send a strong message to your team about how little you care about them.

Considering Abraham Maslow's theory of human motivation (also known as Maslow's hierarchy of needs), right after air, food, and water—all three fundamental to life—comes safety. Without a safe environment, people will consistently fail to reach their potential as individuals and as a team. I have witnessed way too many instances where an executive conveniently turns a deaf ear to a cry for help from a frontline worker being verbally or physically abused by a customer or colleague.

Serving as the president of a hospital and having been married to a clinician for twenty-nine years, I am constantly reminded of how difficult these frontline "tip of the spear" roles can be. Routinely they are very gratifying as care team members watch a patient regain their health, but ever increasingly difficult due to the consumerism mentality so rampant today. Can you imagine how difficult it would be to perform at your peak level with the constant threat of someone believing they can treat you like their personal punching bag simply because they are receiving a service from you?

Clearly, healthcare is a service-oriented industry, but for the care team it should never be mixed martial arts. Nonetheless, you would be amazed at how humans can behave toward one another when under stress. A daily opportunity in any hospital is to pour love and compassion out on a fearful, anxiety-provoking situation. Unfortunately, no matter how much love and compassion are provided, a small percentage of the population will decrease in civility when under stress. Considering the myriad of ways we can demonstrate love for one another, the most fundamental way is to ensure that those we love function in a safe environment.

Several years ago, we instituted a process for de-escalating abusive situations. We ask all members of our team to immediately report any abusive behavior to their supervisor. This person is tasked with having a loving but direct conversation with the offending party. The goal is to address whatever concern led to the poor behavior and to ensure everyone is treated with dignity and respect. More times than not, this simple conversation has been enough to correct the behavior. If the inappropriate behaviors return, a member of our executive team leads a similarly loving but *more* direct conversation about the ramifications of abusive behavior.

One tactic that has been incredibly effective over the years is to read back verbatim any abusive language offered by a customer or colleague. The reaction most people have when hearing their own words repeated to them typically follows: "I don't recall saying that" or complete denial. Still, they receive a brief opportunity to look into a mirror and appreciate how ugly their vile and profane comments can be.

One key to becoming more comfortable with these conversations—because you will never likely be totally comfortable—is to mentally prioritize your impacted team member. If you truly desire excellence in your organization and you genuinely love your team, that should be all the motivation required to discuss the offensive behavior and work toward an amicable situation.

I have had countless experiences with this process. While most of the time the process has worked well, sometimes, even after looking into the mirror, certain people prioritize control over civility and do not seem to care if their behavior harms others.

Language That Would Make a Sailor Blush

One patient thought it would be fine to continuously drop "f-bombs" and other profanities on our team because she was not feeling well. The supervisor for the area followed our process, had a good conversation with her, and the patient's behavior improved for a short while. When her abusive language returned, I personally went to speak with her. After exchanging greetings, I informed her I had been made aware of several instances of her saying "F*** you, b***" to our team members.

She immediately owned her behavior and informed me, "If your nurses don't like sensitive language, they need to work in the nursery."

I replied: "No ma'am. If you want to use that type of language, you will need to find a new hospital. We are going to provide you the best care humanly possible." Pointing to her door, I lovingly yet firmly continued: "Every member of our care team walking through that door must be treated with dignity and respect. In return, we will treat you with dignity and respect. Right now, members of our team are hesitant to enter your room and provide care due to your abusive language. We must have a safe environment for our team to provide the highest level of quality care possible."

Due to her aggressive and repetitious behavior, we ended up firing the patient from our facility and here is why: As leaders, we should prioritize our team by addressing the bad behavior of the 0.1 percent of the population, thus demonstrating love to our team while, at the same time, preserving the highest possible expectations for the care we deliver to the remaining 99.9 percent of the population. This must be our consistent choice versus tolerating inappropriate behavior by the 0.1 percent and have the 99.9 percent experience mediocrity.

LEADERSHIP LESSON

Let that last sentence sink in for a moment. Each day leaders must make decisions to pursue excellence or tolerate mediocrity. The choice is clear. The actions and discipline required to pursue excellence are far more difficult than ignoring a problem and living with average. However, those same efforts that produce excellence are also far more fulfilling than allowing one's life to meander to mediocrity.

The Exorcist

There was another time when the spouse of a patient was leaving scorched earth everywhere she went. Her behavior was addressed, but nonetheless continued. I personally went to visit the patient, who by the way was a saint! He was so complimentary of his care team and so grateful for his treatment. Then there was his wife.

After speaking with the patient for a couple of minutes, I asked his wife who was lying on the sofa how she was doing. She went from passive to full-on Linda Blair in 2.1 seconds! Her countenance literally changed into a hideous scowl as she began to berate me while expressing her grievances.

When she paused to take a breath, I seized the opportunity and informed her, "Part of the reason for my visit today is because I have received numerous reports that you have been treating our team inappropriately."

She aggressively denied any wrongdoing. I pointed out to her that her current behavior was consistent with the reports I had received.

As the patient's wife and I volleyed around "we need to be certain everyone is treated with dignity and respect," I paused and apologized to her husband for the need to have this conversation. The patient literally shrugged his shoulders and said, "I live with it." In that moment, I pictured his wife driving down the road with him in the passenger seat holding up a "HELP ME" sign to passing cars. Unfortunately, with certain people, you just cannot get through.

Making no progress in the conversation, I informed her, "If you are unable to treat our team with dignity and respect, we will be forced to issue a 'no trespass,' and you will have to leave the campus. If you return, you could be arrested."

She assured me that if we went that route their insurance carrier "won't pay you a dime."

In the back of my mind I was thinking, *They already don't pay that well, so where's my motivation*? I kept bringing her back to dignity and respect without which we will never achieve the excellence to which we aspire.

Her parting shot was to say, "I can tell you don't care about me because you don't have valet parking."

With my patience worn thin and in a moment of weakness I replied, "Ma'am, if for no other reason than to prevent you from returning, we will never implement valet parking!"

While I could have admittedly handled that situation with a little more finesse, the legend of that story spread throughout the hospital. A line had been drawn in the sand. Many of our team members expressed never having seen an administrator defend the care team from abusive patients and visitors. Our team began to believe that we did indeed love them and that we cared as passionately for our own people as we did our patients. You cannot begin to imagine the buy-in that generated for our vision to be recognized as one of the best hospitals in the United States.

It has been my experience that many leaders prefer to delegate these difficult conversations or, even worse, avoid them altogether. Too many leaders are more concerned with their patient satisfaction scores than they are with their team member engagement scores. They fail to realize the direct correlation between an engaged care team, happy patients, and great clinical outcomes. Let's face it: the person abusing your team is not likely to give you a strong experience score anyway. All we do by trying to placate their behavior is ensure everyone around them has a terrible experience as well. Consider the ripple effect on your organization by allowing poor behavior to go unchecked. It is exponential!

Leaders should have a sense of personal responsibility to lead these conversations as often as possible for a couple of key reasons. One, you should never ask someone to do something you are not willing to do yourself. Two, it sends a strong message to the entire organization just how serious this priority of loving safety is if the president is willing to get involved and lead the effort.

The hidden beauty is, once you have a few of these conversations and train others how to lead them, issues get resolved before you ever learn about them. That is an incredibly empowering step for your organization. Recently a nursing supervisor informed me of an abusive visitor. I assured her we would address it immediately. She responded, "We already addressed the situation. I just wanted you to be aware." That was an incredibly gratifying moment, knowing the supervisor appreciated and executed on our organizational expectations without asking for permission or for someone else to take the lead. Sheer beauty!

LEADERSHIP LESSON

There is never a better time to lead from the front than when you are protecting the safety of your team. That foundational characteristic of an excellent work environment must be a priority throughout the organization. After the buzz dies down that abuse will no longer be tolerated, that issue, while remaining a key tenet, fades into the background and you are able to focus on other issues, such as delivering impeccable care.

Always remember, we must care as passionately about our people as we do our customers.

9
STOP YELLING

Words. So powerful. They can crush a heart, or heal it. They can shame a soul, or liberate it. They can shatter dreams, or energize them. They can obstruct connection, or invite it. They can create defenses, or melt them. We have to use words wisely.

—J. Brown

Communicating with others is a vital skill set of being a leader. Communicating in a loving and respectful manner is fundamentally vital to being an effective leader.

Either Growing or Decaying

My wife and I got married as soon as we both completed our undergraduate degrees at the ripe old age of twenty-two. We were college sweethearts and very much in love.

However, during our first year of marriage, we fought incessantly. We routinely had arguments that would last for days, with both of us yelling at the top of our lungs! At the beginning of each disagreement, we both activated our full arsenal of "Why you are wrong, and I am right!" diatribes. Often when our argument would seem to be winding down, one of us would invariably bring up an old fight which would reignite our flame of discord and prolong the existing argument another day or so.

As we repeated this behavior for roughly twelve months, one day I paused to reflect and pray about our situation. As I saw it, the fundamental facts about our situation included:

- I love this girl.
- I am going to be with her for the rest of my life.
- We need a more productive process for working out our disagreements.

I had professed my love for her, but my communication style during disagreements was anything but loving, nor was it leading us in a positive direction. As I reflected on the three facts above, the clear direction I received that day was simply, stop yelling. In other words, be respectful in approach, tone, and language. Whenever we disagreed, our emotions and subsequently our tone went straight to nuclear meltdown! This had to stop.

Without saying a word to my wife about this epiphany, over the next few weeks whenever we had a disagreement, I disciplined myself to consistently remain calm and approach the situation from a loving and respectful perspective—no matter what she said. This was not an easy process by any means. My calm demeanor acted like an accelerant for my wife's anger. She would intentionally make statements unrelated to the topic at hand as a means of inciting my emotions. My response, however, was not to act in kind. I lovingly, rationally, and logically ignored the bait of her inciteful comments and brought our attention back to the point we were trying to resolve.

After a few weeks of this routine, my wife asked in a somewhat disappointed tone, "Why don't you yell anymore?" At that point, I shared with her the three points above and the direction I had received. The ensuing conversation melted her heart and forevermore changed how we communicate during disagreements. We have now been married for twenty-nine years. I have often told others that I could count on one hand the number of times we have raised our voices in disagreement toward one another during the most recent twenty-eight years of our marriage.

On a recent fishing trip with our young adult son, we were reflecting on his childhood. He was able to recount three times in twenty years when his mother and I had gotten into intense shouting arguments. Not a bad track record compared to how we started.

LEADERSHIP LESSON

As a side note, some of the best advice I have ever heard about resolving intense arguments was from a minister named Dr. Reggie Weems. His advice is, "When you come to a point of impasse with someone you care about, simply say, 'I am sorry. I was only thinking of myself.'" On the one hand, the humility required to sincerely make that proclamation places all emphasis back on nurturing the relationship. On the other hand, it is incredibly difficult for someone to hear those words and not feel valued. You can work out differences through the process, but your value must be on the relationship.

Too Loud

In over thirty years, there have been two occasions where I yelled at someone with whom I worked. The first instance was at a vendor, who after several months of arduous work undertaken to convert an entire service line of products from a competing vendor, called to say they would not be able to honor the pricing for which we had a signed agreement. In what was essentially a bait-and-switch that had created significant organizational turmoil, the vendor tried to go back on their word. Ultimately, the contract was honored but not without a loss of trust.

The other instance occurred during a construction project at the hospital I was serving. A small fire broke out in the area under construction. The smoke infiltrated the occupied portion of the hospital. Fire alarms were sounding. Caregivers were preparing to evacuate patients. It was a frantic moment. As I called to speak with the construction foreman, he expressed no sense of urgency and began asking unrelated questions. Maybe I could have done something to better communicate the urgency of the situation, but in the moment, I allowed his nonchalant approach to trigger my own frustration.

Make no mistake about it: I have experienced a number of other difficult and intense conversations, but I work to keep the discussion respectful. There have been a few occasions where I have reminded a colleague to maintain a professional and respectful tone. Additionally, you can speak with a level of intensity about a subject and still refrain from entering into a demeaning interaction.

Several years ago, a colleague and I were engaged in a vigorous debate. Early in our relationship, we routinely struggled to see eye-to-eye. We share a similar personality type. We are both focused on excellence, and in all transparency, we are both a little stubborn when we are passionate about a topic. During one of our long discussions, I could tell my friend was becoming agitated. We were at a point of impasse. With all the sincerity I could muster, I told her: "I want you to know, I hear what you are saying, and I appreciate your perspective. I just have a different point of view."

She got a smile on her face and said, "You must be a great husband!"

We both shared a big laugh.

From a leadership perspective, if you are seeking to serve rather than be served, you will consistently make better decisions. In contrast, *self-centered leadership does nothing to enhance the lives of those we serve.* Rather, it inappropriately places the spotlight in the wrong place. Any type of communication that leaves others feeling devalued or disrespected accomplishes little, if anything, in terms of moving the organization forward. Even in situations where someone is being coached for poor performance or even terminated, you never want the recipient to feel demeaned. Otherwise, you have unnecessarily created an enemy.

Additionally, communicating in a loving and respectful manner is by no means an excuse to avoid difficult topics that need to be discussed. On the contrary, if we truly demonstrate love for the person, the team, and the organization, we will have the conversation. With a loving approach, the conversation will inevitably be more productive. This is consistently a better and more effective tactic.

LEADERSHIP LESSON

As related to our voices, volume does not equate to being right. However, volume does equate to our desire to control the discussion by being louder than the other person. When you find yourself in a situation where you want to yell at someone, ask yourself:

- How will yelling help this situation?
- Will yelling improve or worsen our relationship?
- How can I convey my points without yelling?
- Is it time to respectfully step away from this discussion and resume after all the parties have had a moment to cool off?

Your answers to these questions will allow you to intentionally create a better path forward for all involved. Equally as important, you are much more likely to strengthen your relationship with the other party.

10

CONNECTING THE HEAD AND THE HEART

It is only with the heart that one can see rightly;
what is essential is invisible to the eye.
—Antoine de Saint-Exupery

We all carry around technical knowledge between our ears that helps us create value for customers. But technical knowledge is merely half of the equation for excellence. It's the other half that consistently produces excellence: a heart passionate for people. As illustrated in the four-box figure below, this must be a both-and situation, not an either-or matter. Having strong technical knowledge without a passion for serving and caring renders a robotic experience. Conversely, poor technical skills can never be overcome by a great personality. It's strength in both areas that creates the possibility for greatness. The strong combination of the two creates an outcome and experience that is second to none.

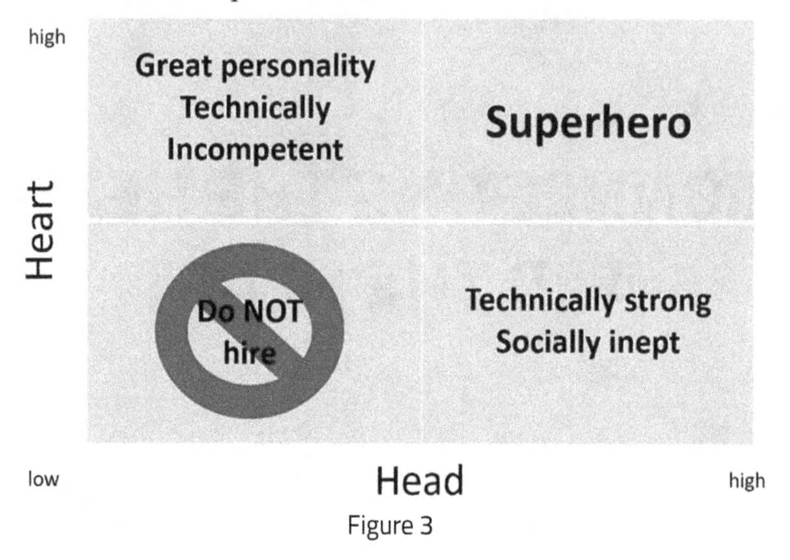

Figure 3

However, ensuring this across larger organizations can become complex. As is the case with most organizations, you will have an array of folks scattered across the spectrum of high head / high heart to low head / low heart. The challenge for leaders is to move existing team members as close to the "Superhero" quadrant as possible through coaching and mentoring, while becoming very stringent on who they hire going forward. We have a phrase for this process: "Love them up or love them out." You cannot tolerate low performance in either of the head-and-heart categories. Instead, you need a both-and mandate that produces both-and results.

Another great tool for coaching and pointing people toward the goal is to highlight excellence whenever you see it. We used to have a "team member of the month" program, but we scrapped it for a couple reasons. First, research indicates those type of programs that honor one person per month can actually be demoralizing to everyone else who is doing a great job. Second, it only allows you to recognize one person per month. If you are a small organization, that might work a little better, but for larger organizations it causes you to miss wonderful opportunities to reinforce the standard to which you aspire.

We chose to implement a program that recognizes any person or team who taps into their discretionary effort bank account to wow a customer. There is no limit on the quantity of people we recognize each month if the quality is there. These team members are widely celebrated throughout the organization as standard bearers. They are the living embodiment of excellence. We tell their stories and place them on the mantle of the organization so everyone knows what type of trophies we are pursuing. We are looking for the type of personnel trophies that make an impact on people's lives, not the type that look good on a résumé for some executive trying to build their career.

We celebrate them in a variety of ways. We use the typical show up to the department with a party cart full of healthy and fun treats so the entire department becomes part of the celebration. We include descriptions of the moment of excellence along with a formal signed certificate of excellence and appreciation. We take pictures of these superheroes and share their stories with the entire facility. Sometimes if we are trying to drive home a particular teaching, we produce a video highlighting the event that led to recognizing them.

To illustrate how contagious this can be, a few years ago our organization implemented a CEO Award program. Out of more than fifty thousand people across our organization, this process annually selects ten people to be highlighted for living out our values. Of the twenty people who have been highlighted in the first two years of the award, nine of them have come from our facility. For perspective, our team represents 2.5 percent of the total population of our health system yet 49 percent of the CEO Award honorees.

One of the best things a leader can do is help others be their best, both individually and collectively. If you do not have a process that recognizes greatness and concurrently teaches the rest of the organization what you are shooting for in terms of this connection between our heads and our hearts, do not miss another opportunity to showcase your best and brightest.

This process of lifting up our superheroes has become one of my most anticipated events every month. The smiles, the surprises, and the goodwill generated when recognizing your team is priceless. The superheroes are doing things worthy of recognition all the time. It is just who they are. Greatness is in their DNA. Highlighting that for the rest of the organization is an incredible teaching moment that underscores your goal.

Real-Life Examples

It is a fortunate event when we get to witness uplifting interactions between our teams and customers. This is especially true when you have team members who feel loved and cared for as they go far beyond the scope of their job description to demonstrate love toward their patients.

A Long Way from Home

In one instance, we had a patient traveling home to a foreign country after visiting family in the United States. The individual had fallen ill and was disoriented when she arrived at the hospital with only the clothes on her back, which were soiled and ruined. Since the plane made an emergency landing for the patient, her luggage and clean clothes were sent on to her final destination.

Rose, a patient care technician, cared for the patient and discovered her unique situation. After Rose's shift, she took the time out of her busy schedule to go buy her patient new pants, shirts, underwear, shoes, and a bag in which to carry her new belongings. In addition to the new items, Rose brought several of her own clothes from home to give to the patient. During this patient's stay, Rose frequently checked on her to make sure she was recovering comfortably.

The night before the patient's discharge, Rose came to the hospital on her day off to help her try on the new items and pick out a special outfit for the plane ride home. The patient, living in an impoverished country, was excited for the new clothes and the "care package" Rose had made for her and her daughter, who was back home.

These acts of kindness were nowhere to be found in Rose's job description, but thankfully they were in her heart.

Being in the Right Place on the Worst Day

Another example of connecting the head and heart that I will never forget occurred in our Emergency Department. A young and seemingly healthy husband suffered a massive heart attack at home and arrived at our facility without a pulse. He was brought to the Emergency Department by ambulance.

His wife came in right after the code blue had been initiated and just sunk onto the nurse's station. Elliott, a unit secretary in the department, was not involved in the code but recognized the wife's grief and asked if she could help. The patient's wife pleaded with her saying, "Just save my husband."

Elliott calmly responded, "I'm not involved in his care, but I know he has a great team caring for him." At that point, Elliott offered to take the patient's wife to a quiet room for more privacy. Once there, instead of leaving, Elliott just sat with the wife and asked if there was anything she could specifically do for her.

The patient's wife simply asked her, "Could you pray with me?"

At that point, Elliott took the wife's hand and began praying with her.

Sadly, her husband did not make it. After the house supervisor worked with the now widow to finalize arrangements, she asked if there was anything else she could do. The widow asked if she could speak with the nurse who greeted her. The supervisor tried to find the "nurse" who ministered to the wife upon her arrival and quickly realized it was Elliott, the unit secretary. The wife said, "Elliott was so kind, brought me into a private room, stayed calm, and prayed for me. There's no way I could have made it through this without her."

Elliott's kindness and compassion are unrivaled. She certainly had her own duties and to-do list that did not include pouring love and compassion into a soon-to-be widow who was filled with fear and grief, but that is what happens when people connect their head and heart: they make the world around them a better place for everyone.

This is also a prime example of the fact that we cannot always provide a curative experience, but we can always provide a healing experience when love and compassion are at the forefront of all we do.

Celebrate Each Moment

Another great example of connecting the head and heart involved an end-of-life cancer patient. A nurse named Ezra learned that the last wish this patient had was to watch her son graduate from high school. Her son had autism and attended a school that could accommodate his educational needs. Ezra realized this patient would not be able to make it to her son's graduation due to her grave condition.

With this in mind, she worked with her team and arranged an in-hospital graduation ceremony and party for the patient's son. The hospice team provided a graduation cap and gown while Ezra spent her own money to buy a cake, balloons, party favors, and a graduation card for the oncology team to sign for the patient and her son. Ezra coordinated all the planning, and the patient was able to have a graduation ceremony and party for her son in her room on the oncology unit.

At the ceremony, Ezra played "Pomp and Circumstance" and presented the son with his hard-earned diploma. The group then enjoyed a graduation party with music, cake, laughter, and fun. This special event brought great happiness and closure to this patient and family. The next day, the patient was discharged home with hospice to spend her final days surrounded by her family.

Ezra is an exemplar when it comes to connecting one's technical knowledge and compassion for others in one beautiful arrangement. These uncommon actions are nowhere to be found in a job description but are the beautiful by-product of superheroes being unleashed to care for others.

God Bless Texas

Yet another shining example of the head-and-heart connection occurred when a patient was brought to our hospital with severe swelling in his lower leg. The swelling was so acute that his pants had to be cut off in the process of his care and were no longer wearable. After a few hours, it was determined that he would be able to be discharged and would be on his way to the airport to return home. Unfortunately, he had no change of clothes with him. He was offered a pair of paper scrubs—the standard response that suffices in most cases. However, Ross, one of our staff, knew we could do better in this situation.

Ross left after his shift and went to a local store to purchase a new pair of pants that would be suitable for the patient's trip. When Ross returned with the clothing, the patient was incredibly grateful and tried to pay Ross for his kind gesture. Ross's response was legendary: "No sir, you don't owe me anything. Welcome to Texas!"

Trophies That Matter Most

I could literally fill a book with examples just like these. The magic that occurs when organizations and leaders create and nurture the right type of environment is worth its weight in gold. In none of these situations was anyone concerned with anything other than doing the right thing for another human being in a time of need.

I love these stories for several reasons, but here are just two. First, love and compassion have the power to change the world around us. Second, none of these acts of love and kindness will ever be listed in a job description, although maybe they should be. However, we are grateful these ideas are in the hearts of our team members. It is our duty as leaders to foster and encourage our team to bring these ideas to fruition through a loving environment.

These are the moments you place on the mantle of the organization. We celebrate these team members as if they had just won an Olympic gold medal. In doing so, we allow celebration to till the ground so more seeds of love will be planted to liberate everyone to pursue the kind of excellence that only comes when people are allowed and encouraged to connect their heads with their hearts.

Over three decades in healthcare, I have never witnessed a patient entering a hospital asking to see the trophy case. They want to know who is going to care for them, who is going to compassionately restore them to health. When your team trusts that all of this "love stuff" is for real, these acts become common place. Part of the process is to encourage your people to be open to interruptions in their day, to those wonderful opportunities to impact someone else's life. We do this in part during the hiring process to ensure people joining our organization know what we celebrate. Sure, it is nice when we have a great financial month or receive some type of recognition, but it is these stories of compassion, above all, that create the great financial months and other recognitions that are a by-product of the environment. The best trophies are not found in a display case but in the actions and subsequent stories of people caring for people in the ways they need. That's what heart-and-head behavior is all about.

LEADERSHIP LESSON

Hire compassionate people who sincerely care about serving others with excellence, then continuously reinforce a culture that turns them loose to demonstrate love to those around them.

When fostering such an environment, it is important to keep an open mind. Some ideas generated by your team will be homeruns, others will be foul balls; both are necessary. Staying with the baseball metaphor, to keep the acts of compassion coming your team needs to keep swinging. A youth baseball coach once advised me when I let a strike go by: "We gave you a bat for a reason. If you want to watch the ball, get a camera for your next at-bat. The picture will last longer." With a little more tact, encourage your team to "swing the bat" and celebrate like crazy when they get a hit. These moments are the trophies you want to display to your team.

11

DEFINE YOUR GOAL AND GET AFTER IT

If you can dream it, you can do it.
—Walt Disney

As I mentioned in chapter one, I made three attempts to get out of healthcare and enter youth ministry full time. My dream of leading hospitals in pursuit of new, ever higher standards was slow to develop. Yet, even with the initial slow pace, I experienced tremendous growth and maturity.

In all three attempts to exit my day job, the door at the church would shut, and within thirty days (you could almost time it), I would receive some type of promotion or additional duties at the hospital. My goal in all of this was simply to do whatever it was that God placed me on this earth to do. And if staying at the hospital fulfilled that, I figured I was doing something meaningful. Shouldn't we all have such aspirations?

Now We Are Getting Somewhere

On the third and final attempt to leave healthcare in favor of youth ministry, I thought the interview had gone extremely well. My wife and I had some serious conversations about downsizing our house and cars given the substantial pay cut I would receive. We had many long logistical discussions on how to best navigate the path financially, but we were mentally bought-in. In fact, we were beyond "bought-in." We were excited about this divinely inspired adventure and all of its implications.

The search committee leader called and invited me to breakfast at a local IHOP on a Thursday morning. I was grateful for the invitation. My wife and I had further discussions about the implications of the meeting. We assumed it was a good prognosis. It clearly meant the interview process would continue. We speculated that maybe the committee had narrowed their list of candidates down to the top two and I was one of them, or maybe they wanted me to come speak. Either way, we took the invitation as good news.

On the morning of our breakfast meeting as we walked to our booth, the committee leader informed me, "Chris, we have narrowed our search down to two candidates, and you are not one of them."

As the shock of that statement jolted me, my initial thought in the next millisecond was, *I don't want to eat pancakes*. My stomach was in a knot!

However, what he shared next was hands down the most encouraging and edifying career conversation I had ever experienced.

He shared that each person on the committee—and that included staffers, parents, and youth—were impressed with my responses to their questions. What they saw and ultimately conveyed in their "rejection" was that I was right where I was supposed to be. The parents on the search team expressed what a better workplace experience they could have if their supervisor approached leadership from a position of love rather than fearmongering.

Even though in the moment I was incredibly disappointed, I remain forever grateful for our conversation. He could have easily said, "You didn't make the cut. We wish you all the best." Instead, he made an investment in another human being that was not going to help him in any way. What a beautiful example of selfless and loving leadership!

Still a bit shocked and disappointed, I tried to relay the information to my wife when I got home. Probably my own fault for playing too many pranks on her, but it took her several minutes before she would believe that I was not moving forward in the interview process.

From that day until now, my goal and passion has been to take the two paths I started on and weave them into one glorious path combining love and leadership, a path that prioritizes people above processes, that values culture over profits. When you prioritize love, people, and values, the inevitable outcome includes leadership, processes, and profits.

LEADERSHIP LESSON

On average, each of us is granted twenty-seven thousand days in our lifetime. Our challenge is to make the most of each moment, each opportunity.

Take advantage of the opportunities in your daily interactions to impact someone's life, to replace fear and anxiety with love and compassion. There are no financial equations associated with such activity, but the rewards for customers, team members, the organization, and even yourself are beyond anything that could ever be captured on a spreadsheet.

Dreaming as a practice can best be done with a clear mind. Go to a place with a great view of the horizon, somewhere you can find solitude and think about what you hope people might say at your eulogy. Then write it out. From that foundation, essentially the person you aspire to be, consider what you would love to accomplish personally and professionally. This is your legacy. Once you articulate your aspirational life accomplishments, begin to work back from there to where you are today in three- to five-year increments. During each iteration, describe what you hope to accomplish, knowing it can change but at least paving a path. With each iteration, be sure to consider what steps you need to take to set yourself up for success for the time segment following it. Once you work back to where you are today, you have created a roadmap to the incredible future you. Now go get it!

Don't Sell Yourself Short

In my late twenties when I began working with Erie Chapman, he encouraged me to go through the process outlined above. Having grown up in a hard-working, blue-collar family, I did not have a great perspective on growth and potential. My mindset at the time was, *If I could eventually report to the president, I will have arrived.* Thankfully, Erie took a long look at my future plans and said, "I think you need to change your focus from reporting to the president to *being* the president." It was a bit shocking to hear those words. They were humbling, challenging, and anxiety provoking all at the same time. No one in my social circles had ever achieved such a role. My parents literally had an expression for people who advanced in life: "They are trying to get above their raising." In other words, be content with your station in life, and do not ever try to better yourself. Thankfully, Erie saw something I could not yet envision.

Given my circuitous route to becoming a hospital president, my timeline was a bit extended. In my goal statement, I set forty-five years of age as the point at which I aspired to become a hospital president. As fate would have it, I turned forty-five the same year I was appointed to my first role as hospital president. Obviously, I would not have realized the life I now live without a change in my mindset.

What needs to change in *your* current mindset to liberate you from the baggage holding you back?

Keep Your Eyes on the Prize

The story of Florence Chadwick provides a lesson we all need to remember. In 1950, she swam twenty-one miles across the English Channel from France to England in thirteen hours and twenty-three minutes. Then, that was the fastest time for any woman completing the task.

One year later, she again swam the English Channel. This time she swam from England to France in sixteen hours and twenty-two minutes. This gave her the distinction of being the only woman to have completed the feat in both directions and setting the standard in record time.

In 1952, Florence attempted to swim the twenty-six miles between Catalina Island and the California coast. As she swam, she was flanked by two small boats to ward off potential shark attacks and to assist her if she could not continue the swim. At roughly fifteen hours into the swim, Florence began to doubt herself. A thick fog had set in, making visibility difficult. As she began to express doubt, she swam another hour before succumbing to fatigue. Unable to see the shoreline due to the dense fog, she asked to be pulled from the water. As she began to recover and reorient herself, she and the crew realized she was within one mile of her goal.

Two months later, she attempted the swim again. Once again, she experienced a dense fog. This time she retained a mental image of the coastline and was successful in reaching her goal.

LEADERSHIP LESSON

Leadership requires vision and imagination. Blocking out rate-limiting environmental factors can be challenging, but it is a requisite to realize your potential.

What environmental factors are holding you back from bringing your dreams to fruition?

What mental models do you hold to be true that simply need to be smashed for you to flourish?

Become adept at recognizing and rejecting limiting ideology. After all, it was likely created by someone unwilling to do the work or afraid to push their limits.

12

LOVE *IS* THE STRATEGY

Love is life. All, everything that I understand, I understand only because I love. Everything is, everything exists, only because of love.
—Leo Tolstoy

Everything we do should start and end with the premise "Love one another." While as leaders we will have a number of market strategies and operational tactics, a loving foundation sets us up to maximize our potential. That simple principle calls us and challenges us to bring the best we have to offer. It compels us to higher standards in our work, in our relationships, in our commitments . . . in everything.

Believe me, I have had more than my fair share of skeptics when I tell them everything we do should start and end with "love one another." I have reassured them that if we focus on our culture, how we care for one another, how we raise expectations around our interactions with one another, the metrics will follow. The incredible trend lines after which most people seek will become a by-product of the degree to which we love one another.

I Thought You Were Full of It

After having worked together for a couple of years, an exceptionally talented chief financial officer shared with me, "I remember when you started talking about all of that love stuff. How the outcomes would follow."

I asked her, "What were you thinking initially?"

She responded, "I thought you were full of it."

Even a numbers-oriented CFO came to appreciate how a loving culture produces superior outcomes.

At one point, after a couple of high-profile meetings where I reiterated to various leaders and board members how we were going to implement a loving culture, my well-intended boss pulled me to the side and suggested, "You might lighten up on all of the culture talk." I appreciated where he was coming from, but in my mind I was thinking, *That is the most important thing we should be talking about!* To his credit, he provided space for me to lead. Within a few short months, he was very encouraged with the results being driven by our burgeoning culture. Metrics across the board were experiencing tremendous improvement. Why? Because we began creating an experience and associated outcomes that both providers and consumers wanted.

It is completely reasonable for well-educated leaders who have been trained in business schools or by people who went to business school to be uncomfortable, skeptical, or even obstinate with talk about and the promotion of the concept of a loving culture as a strategy. Business schools do not teach about love, much less love as the focal point of culture and strategy. It was several years after obtaining my MBA and launching my career before I heard anyone mention love as a business concept. However, the results of that focus are undeniable.

The challenge is to appreciate that a loving culture as your *primary strategy* is superior to a traditional approach of writing nice mission, vision, and values statements and still failing to care for your team and customers as the foundation of all you do. As a leader, you would not accept a team member who provided a mediocre effort. Why should you tolerate a mediocre working environment? Whatever your organization's environment is, it will heavily dictate outcomes. You should never tolerate an environment that promotes anything short of excellence.

Unfortunately, that is not how most leaders are trained. It is much easier and certainly more comfortable to focus on trend lines, spreadsheets, ratios, and workflows, all of which are important but not the most important. Sadly, as a society of leaders, our priorities have eroded into a short-term fixation on profitability. This myopic approach prevents us from remaining focused on the fundamental value proposition—namely, that culture consistently drives outcomes, because in industries requiring human interaction, people drive value.

From an organizational standpoint, we are routinely challenged to do more and be better with less. At some point we run into the law of diminishing returns, which means once we have maximized our potential through a given approach or process, additional improvement efforts will begin yielding fewer results. To be clear, we should be engaged in improvement efforts, but as a complimentary approach to loving one another.

If, from this perspective, we chase our true potential, we will routinely surpass aggressive goals. We are far better off chasing our best than chasing a number, a trend line, or a trophy. Most people are not going to be terribly motivated or inspired by chasing a metric; it is impersonal and inanimate. Instead, challenge yourself to be your best as an expression of love for your team, your customer, and your community. That is a completely different source of inspiration and motivation, and it's personal and living.

Dead Serious

While orienting to a new role, I did the usual. I got to know people and the organization. What I saw was a number of people who feared losing their job due to poor facility financial performance. There is a saying in management engineering: "Volume covers a multitude of sins." Basically, if you have enough volume, it can cover up some operational or leadership shortcomings. However, before you can achieve volume growth, you must consistently provide a superior product. To provide a superior product, you must have strong operational and leadership processes.

One characteristic every hospital or any other organization should want to be known for is high quality. Our hospital was known for average quality based upon a national benchmarking process. On a scale of one to five, one being the lowest and five being the highest rating, we were a three. The hospital I had just left went from being a three to a five in three years. The new organization was a bigger hospital and hence a bigger task. Nonetheless, I asked our director of quality improvement to develop a gap analysis between where we were and where we wanted to be. Again, if you love your patients, you should want the absolute best for them.

Our director prepared a solid, well thought out presentation for our senior leadership team. I say "solid" because she developed a plan to improve our rating from a three to a four. While there is nothing wrong with a stepwise plan, I paused the presentation to express my appreciation for her efforts and then inquired, "Where is the plan for us to deliver our best and thereby achieve a rating of five?" She politely informed me, the "new guy," that she felt we were a few years away from being a level five facility. What I had found, however, is that the amazing thing about people and teams is if you place them in the right environment, they can do so much more than we typically ever imagine.

Following her presentation, we planned a leadership think tank for our larger team. We call it a think tank because I loathe the term "retreat" and feel most leaders do not take enough time to think about the future—what we want to be when we grow up. At this session, we discussed the negative connotation with change. It can be uncomfortable, it can be disruptive, and it can bring loss. That said, we were in a comfort zone filled with mediocrity. Many leaders were fearful of making mistakes, while others were working feverishly to stay below the radar.

We discussed several beautiful thoughts by change agents:

- George C. Lichtenberg: "I cannot say whether things will get better if we change; what I can say is they must change if they are to get better."

- Albert Einstein: "The world as we have created it is a process of our thinking. It cannot be changed without changing our thinking."
- Harold Wilson: "He who rejects change is the architect of decay."
- John Kenneth Galbraith: "Faced with the choice between changing one's mind and proving that there is no need to do so, almost everyone gets busy on the proof."
- Mother Teresa: "I alone cannot change the world, but I can cast a stone across the waters to create many ripples."
- Winston Churchill: "To improve is to change; to be perfect is to change often."

We also discussed how growth occurs outside of our comfort zone when we are stretched and pressed to grow and become better at our craft. With this as an encouragement to get out of our comfort zone of average and embrace a sincere love for one another, our team, our patients, and our communities, we began to lay out a twenty-four-month vision that would place us on a path to become one of the best hospitals in the United States. We were not after a trophy. Rather, we wanted to change as an expression of love for what we do and how we do it.

A couple of weeks went by and an opportunity for improvement came up in one of our daily leadership huddles. I took the opportunity to remind everyone of the journey to excellence we committed to by asking, "Twenty-three months from now, when we are one of the best hospitals in the United States, what will that process and outcome look like?" I could tell minds went back to our think-tank session.

One manager was bold enough to share with me: "I really appreciate you reminding us of our commitment. When you referenced twenty-three months from now, a lot of us were thinking, 'Oh, he's serious about this!'"

And that I was.

By-Products of Transformation

Eighteen months after our initial think tank, I had taken a vacation and was sitting on a beach with my wife. I will never forget receiving the email from our director of quality improvement informing me we had just received national recognition as a level five hospital for quality outcomes! From average to truly one of the best hospitals in the United States in just eighteen months! The fundamental change in performance was how we approached one another and our work together.

We held a big celebration to honor our care team—the people who made this change happen. Interestingly, Erie shared with me after the fact that he thought that moving from a level three to a level five hospital in that brief time frame was far too aggressive. I laughingly thanked him for not sharing that with me beforehand.

When an organization's culture is based upon this principle of loving one another, key things occur:

- The organization figures out how to best express love and care for its team. What would that look like in your organization? Aside from a paycheck, which must be earned, what was the last thing your organization did to go above and beyond to express love to its team?
- Team members in turn are focused on respecting the dig-

nity and self-worth of each individual.

- Fear of failure becomes a thing of the past.
- People are liberated to be their best.
- We stop chasing trophies and start chasing perfection with every interaction. As football great Vince Lombardi said, "Perfection is impossible," yet it remains an exciting target! Who cares if we do not hit perfection? Yet, as an organization, we will go much further along that journey if it remains our pursuit.
- We celebrate. Not celebrating trophies, although there will be many. Instead, we celebrate the expressions of love that create ever higher standards. Specifically, we celebrate milestones, and we celebrate without being satisfied that we have finally arrived at perfection. The way you celebrate underscores what is important to the organization. It also reinforces the culture you espouse.
- Our thirst for better is never quenched. Despite that, we have a tremendous amount of fun along the way. All the while setting higher and higher standards for ourselves and hopefully for our industry.

LEADERSHIP LESSON

Former politician, author, and motivational speaker Les Brown encouraged us, "Shoot for the moon. Even if you miss it you will land among the stars." I would much rather chase a lofty goal and fall short of it than not be challenged and succeed at something much less. When love dominates motivations and interactions, the absence of fear provides the freedom to dream big and execute with passion.

13

WE ARE ALL DIFFERENT

Our ability to reach unity in diversity
will be the beauty and the test of our civilization.
—Mahatma Gandhi

Growing up in a predominately Caucasian area of Ohio during the 1970s and '80s, ours was a Christian home, but it was, at best, prejudicial toward minorities.

I vividly recall walking into a restaurant as a young child and seeing an interracial couple enjoying a meal just beyond the hostess stand. The gentleman was African American, and the lady was Caucasian. The gentleman was facing the entrance, and the lady had her back to us. Seeing the couple, my father began expressing his disgust with their relationship loud enough for everyone to hear. I recall looking at the expression on the gentleman's face as he dropped his gaze to the food in front of him, never raising his head and never offering a retaliatory word. I will never forget the expression on the gentleman's face and the feeling I had as a young boy. I was embarrassed by my father's comments and saddened by the man's expression.

Later in high school, I was working a summer job and ended up asking out one of my coworkers who just so happened to be South Korean. Once my mother found out the young lady was not Caucasian, I received an extended lecture on how interracial relationships were forbidden in the Bible.[5] My mother literally forbade me from going on the date. When I called to cancel our date, the young lady knew why without me telling her. It broke my heart to hear her cry because of pain inflicted upon her due to my parents' ignorance.

To provide some insight as to how my parents grew up, when my wife and I were engaged, I wanted to take her to meet my grandparents. Both of my grandmothers still lived in the rural community in Appalachia where my parents grew up. We stopped in the little town to give my wife a feel for the place. As we walked down the sidewalk, my wife and I were shocked to see what was on the front page of the local newspaper. The above-the-fold headline was promoting a Ku Klux Klan rally—not denouncing it but promoting it! The year was 1989.

After earning a football scholarship to attend college, I met more African American people than I had ever known in my life up to that point. I will never forget my first game as starting line-backer. It was an away game during my sophomore year. On the trip, I was sharing a room with a talented freshman named Al, who happened to be black. Our coach had asked me to look out for Al as needed. That night before our 10 p.m. curfew, I pulled out my playbook to review defensive schemes, assignments, blitz packages, and so on. As Al got into his bed, he began to read his Bible. In that moment I thought, *Who is mentoring whom?* I had a good game the next day, but Al provided a great example of character and leadership. He is one of the best human beings I have ever known.

Later in life as our family was discussing race, I assured my father that if I ever had a daughter, I would be honored if she were fortunate enough to marry someone like Al. Even though my comments were not received with open arms, it did not change the fact that Al is that great of a guy. Through my college experience, being exposed to people from diverse backgrounds and cultures was one of the greatest learning opportunities ever.

The good news in all of this is that after years of talking with my parents, they have come around. I am not saying we see eye-to-eye on all things related to race and equality, but considering how they were raised in that rural Appalachian community, they have grown tremendously, and their hearts have softened toward people who may not look like them. When I think about how my parents grew up versus how our son has been raised, our family tree has flipped from prejudice to peace, from bigotry to benevolence, in two generations. All it takes is a focus on loving your neighbor as yourself. It really is that simple.

Safety for All

Serving as the president of one of the best hospitals in the United States, a key part of my role is to care for the people who care for the patients. This includes everything from ensuring our team has the right equipment to promoting a healthy work environment where people can excel at what they have been called to do. As noted earlier, the foundation for a healthy environment begins with safety. The premise of safety mandates that we protect our care team when people become rude and discourteous. Our hospital is a place of healing. There is no room for inappropriate behavior. We fully appreciate that, for many people coming to the hospital, they find it an anxiety provoking experience. We also fully appreciate the fact that our best can only be delivered in a loving and peaceful environment. Finally, we appreciate that there is a small group of people in any society who, no matter how much love and compassion you show them, insist on treating those around them poorly.

Stop the Line

Twenty-nine days after the death of George Floyd, we were in our weekly senior leadership meeting. One of our leaders received a text message that a visitor was upset about our limited visitation policy related to the Covid-19 pandemic. The visitor asked to speak with someone from the administration.

To honor the request, our incredibly talented patient safety officer, who happens to be African American, went to address the visitor's concerns. Upon greeting her, the Caucasian visitor promptly announced: "You're not administration. I want to speak with someone who's white!"

The next text message conveyed in our meeting was that the visitor asked to speak with a "white person." It felt like we had instantly been transported to the year 1960! Immediately, I left our meeting and went to the entrance to address the situation. On the way, I ran into our patient safety officer (PSO). In a completely calm manner, she provided a synopsis of the interaction.

As we approached the visitor, I introduced myself. She instantly attempted to dismiss our PSO. I assured her that it was perfectly fine for our leader to be involved in the conversation. At that point, I asked the visitor, "Did you seriously request to speak with a 'white person'?"

She didn't hesitate to own her reprehensible behavior and replied, "Yes I did! You also need to know you have black nurses on the floors taking jobs from whites!"

Much like in manufacturing, in healthcare when there has been a safety breach, this was a stop-the-line moment! After the immediate shock of her statement, I ended the conversation and issued her a verbal "no trespass" and directed her to leave the campus. We followed up with a letter of relationship termination, which directs the individual to refrain from returning to our campus. You cannot have a healing environment if you attempt to coddle or placate abusive behavior.

After things settled down, I went to check on our PSO. When I asked her, "How are you doing?" she responded in a surprisingly calm manner, "I'm fine"—as if what had just taken place was no big deal. Her response caused me to wonder if she had been conditioned to deal with this kind of event through similar encounters over the course of her life.

Regardless, I commit to providing her and all our team members with a safe environment, which inherently leads to some of the best care on the planet. We shared this story with our entire team during virtual town hall sessions to reiterate our commitment to being part of the solution as it relates to diversity, equity, and inclusion for everyone.

Additionally, we formed a Called to Love Council to help guide our local efforts. During our second meeting, every nurse in the room shared stories of patients and family members requesting staffing changes driven by racism. Once again, we shared with our team that we will never comply with race-based requests. One of the nurses shared how she felt abandoned by her supervisor who complied with such a request when a patient proclaimed, "I hate all Muslims and want you out of my room now!" In that moment, she decided if our organization ever supported another racist request, she would simply leave.

Stop the Line Consistently

More recently, I received a late evening text from a hospital supervisor that read: "Family member very abusive. Refusing black caregivers. Heading there now with security."

When I arrived at the hospital, our supervisor was consoling two African American team members who were holding back tears. I hugged them, apologized for the ignorance to which they had been subjected, and assured them it would be addressed.

Upon initiating a conversation with the family member, he denied having said he did not want blacks caring for his wife. I informed him three people heard him make the statement. He then acknowledged, "Well, I said it, but that's not what I meant." When I told him there is only one way for that statement to be interpreted, he tried to assure me he was not racist, and he even had black friends. I was tempted to ask if any of his "friends" had ever been to his house for dinner or if he had been to theirs, but I refrained. This stop-the-line moment also ended with a no trespass.

We share these examples of racism because they happen far more often than we realize. Caucasian colleagues have gone so far to express, "I cannot imagine something like this happening in my organization," or "Before you shared this, I honestly did not believe racism existed." We also share them because we, as leaders, should never settle in pursuit of a safe and equitable environment for our team members.

Shortly after we began shedding light on these situations, I received the following email from one of our care team members.

> *Dear Chris,*
> *Thank you for advocating for minorities and colored team members like me. It made me teary-eyed watching and listening to your latest town hall meeting. It is a lullaby to my ears knowing that my leader has my back and who does not tolerate racial injustice in any form or fashion. For that I thank you from the bottom of my heart and on behalf of my beautiful mother who is thousands of miles away anxious that her daughter is in a foreign country rendering service to mostly non-Orientals who do not speak the same language as her daughter. You inspire me to continue to care for patients and coworkers with love and compassion, and to even further my loyalty to this great organization.*
> *Always grateful for your support.*

There will never be a trophy or certification that will compare to knowing you made a difference in the life of a person who has experienced hateful discrimination solely because of their skin tone, their faith, or any other differentiator.

LEADERSHIP LESSON

In a respectful and loving environment, there is no room to placate racism. In a loving society, there is no space to coddle hatred. As Dr. Martin Luther King Jr. said: "Darkness cannot drive out darkness; only light can do that. Hate cannot drive out hate; only love can do that." Given that hate is taught, we as leaders should be about the business of teaching love through every word or deed that emanates from our existence.

Unity through Love and Learning

In my early thirties, I was serving as vice president for a health system in Tennessee. Part of my responsibilities included the surgical suites. One day while walking toward the operating room control desk, I heard a loud commotion. The disruption was two male nurses yelling at one another, clearly on the verge of fisticuffs. Inquiring about their disagreement, I learned that Bill, a Caucasian nurse—who was the "class clown" of the Operating Room—had made a completely inappropriate and insensitive comment to Ivory, an African American nurse, that led to their altercation. In a terrible attempt to be funny, Bill said to Ivory, "Don't you think it's ironic for a black guy to be named Ivory?"

Trying to maintain a calm environment in a patient care area, I asked both men to join me in my office. Fortunately, I knew them both as men of faith. We sat in my office with the chairs arranged in a triangle. Both men shared what had happened. As Ivory shed tears sharing the years of pain that he and members of his family had suffered due to racism in their community, Bill was crying due to his own ignorant insensitivity and for having added to Ivory's pain. It was an intense and powerful emotional exchange between the two men. Thirty minutes earlier, they had been standing at the team station on the verge of a fight. (By the way, both men were over six feet tall and more than two hundred pounds each. I was not interested in trying to break up a fight that day!) Fast forward thirty minutes and all three of us were in my office crying at various points trying to seek reconciliation.

For his part, Bill knew what he did was wrong. At points during the conversation, he sobbed uncontrollably over the emotional injury he had inflicted on a person he considered to be a friend. After a sincere apology, Ivory was equally up to the task of forgiving and disconnecting Bill from the racism he had experienced in his life. By the end of the conversation, both men were crying and hugging it out, with Bill continuously apologizing, Ivory continuously forgiving, and both proclaiming the other as "brother." This was a beautiful example of love being so much more powerful than hate or ignorance.

The challenge we all face is being vulnerable and intentional about allowing love to flow from our lives.

14

"YOU CAN'T ALWAYS LOVE THEM"

Somewhere between love and hate lies confusion, misunderstanding and desperate hope.
—Shannon L. Alder

The title of this chapter is a direct quote from an executive who was referencing a situation that needed to be improved. Everyone in the meeting agreed improvement was a must. With the acknowledgment that performance in a particular area needed to get better came those unbelievable words, "You can't always love them." The comment was intended to convey, *You need to be hard on this group of people to get them to do what you want them to do.* As if these team members who were diligently working in an environment perfectly designed to produce the substandard outcomes we were experiencing would perform better if we yelled at them or told them how lousy they were as human beings. Sadly, for workers around the world, far too many leaders subscribe to this mentality of what it means to lead. To the contrary, successful leaders who lead with love will not only address demanding situations, they will also do it in a respectful manner that inspires people to go above and beyond routine expectations.

There are several elements to leading such a loving, respectful conversation, but three key ingredients stick out. First, *our mindset is our foundation.* It is easy to fall into the mental trap of approaching improvement opportunities with frustration: "Why isn't this person or team doing what they are supposed to do?" or "Why are these people making my life so difficult?" This self-centered mental trap quickly leads to a "my way or the highway" discussion. Instead, imagine if every improvement discussion had begun with the simple assumption, "I am confident this team wants to achieve greatness." Several good things happen when you flip that mental model, most notably:

- You will do a much better job analyzing the situation.
- The people you are depending on to deliver value to your customers will sense you are for them, not against them.
- This will improve openness to discuss and more importantly take ownership of the challenge in question.
- Pretty soon, with little effort, you will experience alignment.

Next, *if our mentality sets the table, our approach cooks the meal.* With that, we must clearly define with as much data as possible where *we* are and where *we* want to be. The delta in that equation is our opportunity, but the "we" in that message is the most important variable. No one enjoys following a leader who only shows up for accolades. Therefore, it is paramount for leaders to articulate ownership just as much, if not more so, than every other member of the team. This is another way in your daily activity to convey you care about the team and that you are in the foxhole with them.

In college, our football team experienced a coaching change my freshman year. At a young age, it was an interesting contrast in leadership styles. The first coach always assumed the blame for anything that went wrong. If we suffered a loss, it was his fault for not preparing us better. When we won, he consistently placed the credit on the players and assistant coaches. During winter break, through misalignment with administration, he resigned and went on to successfully lead another program for a couple of decades. Unfortunately, his replacement was the exact opposite when it came to assuming responsibility or sharing credit. When we lost, he would call out assistant coaches and players on his weekly television show for having done a poor job. When we won, it was all due to his master strategy.

For those of us who had experienced both leadership styles, the coaching situation was eye-opening. We players would joke that we would walk through fire for the first coach, but with the second coach we would not even urinate on him if he were on fire. Alignment matters. Being committed to one another in good times and bad times matters. Not surprisingly, the first coach lasted decades longer as a head coach and had a much better win-loss ratio because his teams knew he loved them.

Finally, *after improvement tactics have been agreed upon and implementation has begun, loving leadership compels us to stay in touch with the team and the outcomes of the new process*. This continues to be a respectful conversation. There will be times when celebrations are called for, and there will be times to repeat this three-step cycle, but by no means should a leader ever feel the need to engage in disparaging the people who are called upon to create value.

Our mindset dictates the leadership path we follow.

Instead of This . . .	Consider This . . .
They do not care.	What elements of the current system are preventing us from producing top decile outcomes?
Some heads are going to roll.	What needs to be done to ensure everyone can be successful?
It is time to fish or cut bait.	How can I support you?
Why will they not do what they are told?	Does everyone understand their role and interdependencies with other roles and teams?

This list could be infinite, but the main takeaway is to be affirming to the team, clear on expectations, and consistent in approach. Deviations from this process can and will erode trust among the team. As a leader, people watch intently to be certain your words and deeds match. Hold yourself to the same standard, if not a higher one, to which you want others to be accountable to. Anything less and your message of excellence becomes diluted and frail.

Mr. Teflon

With this approach in mind, not everyone will respond the same. Several years ago I knew a director named Craig. He was incredibly talented, but he was also very satisfied with avoiding ownership of difficult situations. When we began working together, it became clear that Craig, especially on improvement efforts, struggled having loving accountability conversations. His approach to improvement opportunities was avoidance, which is a common response. His approach also reminded me of the adage that the easy way out typically leads back in.

Shortly after we began working together, our leadership team was facing another challenging budget. When is that not the case, right? After extensive and sometimes intense discussions, we finally agreed on several tactics that would allow us to get to where we needed to be. We also agreed that "we" as a leadership team would own these efforts and accordingly developed a communication plan for the rest of the team. Within forty-eight hours, a manager who reported to Craig requested a meeting with me. As we sat down, Fran's opening comments were, "Craig told me this is what you want me to do." Given the conversation we had just two days earlier about leading with ownership, I asked Fran to clarify her comment. She affirmed, "Craig told me this is what Chris wants us to do." Craig was not taking ownership, even though he had agreed to.

To say I was disappointed in Craig's approach would be an understatement. I would have felt much better about speaking with Fran to gain clarity if Craig had taken ownership. Unfortunately, he had obviously walked out of the meeting with our leadership team and immediately washed his hands of the work ahead. So I had a respectful yet direct conversation with Craig about the incontrovertible link between leadership and ownership. As was his preference, Craig tried to avoid ownership of the direction he had given Fran. Subsequently, he and I had some mentoring sessions to ensure we were on the same philosophical page from a leadership standpoint. Through these conversations, he grew as a leader and went on to be promoted twice before leaving the organization for a larger growth opportunity. Initially, his ownership in challenging situations was a glaring weakness. To his credit, he flipped his approach and made it a strength.

That said, it would have been easy to bring Craig in after his lack of ownership and simply let him go. This happens all the time. It also creates organizational unrest, erodes trust, and leads to a toxic environment. As we discussed earlier, there are times when people actively make decisions to do the wrong thing for whatever reason. In those moments, it is perfectly fine and routinely healthy for all parties to allow someone to re-enter the job market. But to anyone who believes "You can't always love people," please tell me when you should *stop* loving people! To the contrary, one of the most effective ways to change the aberrant behavior of a person is to love them. Leaders become challenged in living this value out when they value profits more than people.

LEADERSHIP LESSON

Gains and losses can become infectious. Your leadership choice to love people or to treat them as a commodity heavily influences the extent to which people will follow you.

Additionally, the misunderstanding that love is always warm and fuzzy and only has positive connotations is incredibly short-sighted when considering the depth and breadth of loving leadership. Love is always the best answer, especially during the tangential challenges associated with an improvement opportunity.

15

LANGUAGE MATTERS

When someone loves you, the way they talk about you is different. You feel safe and comfortable.
—Jess C. Scott

How we view people directly influences how we refer to them and how we interact with them. How we interact with people has a direct impact on our relationship with them and all the by-products of that relationship.

Cherished

If I were to hand you my phone and ask you to call my wife, you would not find her in the normal alphabetical listing for her name. You would need to look for the title I gave her long ago, "Princess." This started over thirty-three years ago when we were just dating. I still view her this way, which influences how I treat her and drives so much about our relationship.

Similarly, if you want to drive engagement and alignment, how you view, refer to, and treat people matters immensely. Fundamentally, most people work to pay bills, have some fun, and hopefully save a little for retirement. While on a base level we are all employees, one of the many goals of loving leadership is to create an environment where people can earn a living, but more importantly, live out a calling. The difference between these two states cannot be overemphasized.

In the first environment you have employees showing up to exchange labor for wages. This is a tough existence wrought with every imaginable obstacle to success. This is where most people perform to their job description and nothing more. Basically, they do what they need to so they can remain gainfully employed and pay their bills. Extra effort rarely occurs in the "employee" model.

In the second environment—the aspirational environment—you have people engaged on a more purposeful level, connecting the dots between what we do and why we do it. In this space, people going above and beyond the call of duty is so routine that it becomes a cultural norm. This is the difference between what must be done (job description orientation) and what could be done (team orientation). Much like discretionary income, the holder gets to decide if it is spent and specifically how it is spent.

Over the years, I have become a big believer in the importance of language. Therefore, I prefer the term "team member" versus "employee" or "staff." I have known organizations who use other terms, such as "colleague" or "associate," to move their organization beyond the "employee" mentality.

Several years ago, I was discussing this issue with an executive who was new to our organization. His reasonable assessment was along the lines of "I get what you are trying to do, but I have seen other organizations that call their employees something nice but still treat them terribly."

I responded to the executive's fair comment with: "I could not agree with you more. That is exactly why we set out to change the culture of this organization—to align it with how we view and treat people—before we ever considered changing our terminology."

If you view the intentional use of language as an "idea of the month," you are doomed for failure. Attitude and action must align with and often precede the "official" terminology. This executive's legitimate concern for calling people something that conveys respect and affection while treating them poorly also conveys an organization's identity and integrity issues. As is so often the case, actions must precede words, otherwise the words are empty, and you do more harm than good in terms of engaging and aligning your team.

For these reasons and likely due to the influence of my athletic background, I personally prefer use of the term "team member." For anyone who has ever been a member of a team, there is a sense of connection to something bigger than oneself. There is a sense of "we" versus "me." There is an inherent need for vulnerability, interdependency, and trust. There is a higher focus on the responsibility that goes along with being a member, and the need to fulfill your duties to your best ability. The team is counting on you, just as you are counting on the team.

Translating this thought into your organization is a matter of setting your team as your number one priority, not number one *after* customer satisfaction, not number one *after* profitability. Your team must be number one, period! Everything else flows from this singular focus. When your people know this about you, they know how you prioritize them—and this matters immensely.

If I call my wife "Princess" and forget her birthday or our anniversary or to simply cherish her daily, she will know I have failed to prioritize her and our relationship. As poet and writer Maya Angelou said, "I've learned that people will forget what you said, people will forget what you did, but they will never forget how you made them feel." How people feel after interacting with you is largely driven by how you prioritize them.

On a hierarchy level, the term "staff" is also a pet peeve. I have witnessed too many people in formal leadership positions use this term in a pejorative manner to imply "Those beneath me." When rolling out the communication plan for a new project, I witnessed one executive say, "How are the rank and file going to understand this?" Rank and file? Are you kidding me? That is a leader with an exacerbated sense of self. On a fundamental level, he didn't grasp that we are *all* leaders, and we are *all* staff.

In the first hospital where I served as president, after we respectfully changed how we referred to one another, members of our team began to evaluate other terms commonly used in our facility. Terms like "psych patient" and "frequent flier" are commonplace in the healthcare industry. We decided more respectful terms would be "behavioral health patients" and "routine guests." These nuances may seem small, but if they stem from your core belief that we are called to love others, they become powerful milestones on your journey to excellence. Additionally, in the vein of receiving feedback, our team was comfortable correcting another team member if they ever slipped and used one of the less respectful terms.

If you are still questioning the power of language, ask yourself if you would prefer an employee or a team member provide healthcare to the person whom you love the most on this planet. Picture your loved one's face in your mind. Would you want the person you love treated as a diagnosis or a disease process? Or would you prefer they receive world-class care for their disease process while being compassionately cared for in the manner befitting your love for them?

LEADERSHIP LESSON

Language conveys care, it renders respect, and it proliferates priorities. Take time to examine the language you use when interacting with others. Does your language communicate love for others or is it self-aggrandizing? Prioritizing others through your language will always yield better results as you exalt and encourage those around you.

16

LEADING IN CRISIS

Fear is not the solution to a situation.
It is the alarm bell. Figuring out what to do
about the alarm bell is what you need to focus on.
—Mark McLaughlin

When the coronavirus first came to the United States and specifically our market, the first two weeks were without question the most challenging of my career. We were learning new information daily. We were trying to determine how virulent and how deadly the virus could be. Hundreds of policy changes were made at lightning-fast pace. With safety as our top priority, there were more questions than answers. During those two weeks, we worked around the clock to get answers. In the meantime, we made the best decisions we could with the information we had. Thankfully, we were not overrun with Covid-19 cases during that time. It took a few months before we saw a substantial rise in cases. While the slow rise in volume was a blessing we would later come to appreciate, it did not take away from the fear, the anxiety, or the unknowns of the situation.

Key Pillars

Two core competencies that aided us during this crisis were extreme flexibility and intense communication. One day we were being told that we should never reuse an N95 mask. The next day we were being told that we must reuse our N95, and we were buying ultraviolet lights to sanitize the masks. This shift was driven by the rapid spread of the pandemic and the subsequent impact on the global supply chain to deliver the much-needed personal protective equipment (PPE). This drove anxiety through the roof.

You do not educate, train, and create policies for a highly focused, intelligent, science-oriented group of people in one thought pattern their entire career and then do a complete one-hundred-eighty-degree turn overnight and expect them to feel comfortable about the process. This was truly a situation of we may not have what we want but we must make the best of what we have. I will never forget jumping on surprise Friday evening supply chain calls to be informed, "We are not certain if we have enough masks to get you through the weekend." Adequate supply or not, I knew that our patients were not going anywhere, and we still had a team to protect from this deadly virus.

As it related to communication, a belief I have always operated under is, in the absence of facts, people create their own reality. Sometimes that will even happen in the *presence* of facts, depending on the individuals involved and how chaotic the situation may be. This is a prime example of how perception creates reality. Managing the perception of key stakeholders through timely and recurrent information is paramount, and it is 100 percent the responsibility of leaders.

Throughout the pandemic, we deployed a multipronged approach. Given the challenge of minimizing human contact, we used daily emails and supplemented them with video messages from various leaders. We quickly adopted virtual town halls, which allowed for better interaction related to question-and-answer sessions. This process and cadence came to generate quite a following, even among healthcare providers who did not work on our campus. As time went on and the situation became more stable, we reduced the frequency to ensure the messaging remained impactful.

In a joint video message with our chief nursing officer and myself, one care provider commented: "I love the way you all present things in a calm, matter-of-fact way. If mom and dad are calm, the kids will be calm." While we had plenty of stressful moments, primarily around keeping our team and patients safe, delivering calm communication helped ease tensions.

Leadership Attention

While working with Erie Chapman, one day we were walking out of a meeting and a colleague came running into the suite yelling, "A man was just shot on the corner no more than a hundred feet from where we were standing!"

With little deliberation, Erie calmly said, "Well, this is going to require some leadership attention." Then he briskly walked into his office and began orchestrating safety measures.

I will never forget his demeanor in responding to a shooting right outside our doors. In a tragic situation, he provided a sense that everything was going to be okay. In the moment, even if things are going to get worse, it does not help the situation for leaders to panic.

Without clear and calm communication, flexibility is a long shot at best. The Navy SEALs have an ethos that in part states:

> I serve with honor on and off the battlefield. The ability to control my emotions and my actions, regardless of circumstance, sets me apart from others. Uncompromising integrity is my standard. My character and honor are steadfast. My word is my bond. We expect to lead and be led. In the absence of orders, I will take charge, lead my teammates, and accomplish the mission. I lead by example in all situations. I will never quit. I persevere and thrive on adversity.

While theirs is a more violent theatre, most of us will face chaos at some point. The extent to which we lead in a calm and focused manner will directly impact those who follow and their demeanor.

Cocky?

Earlier in my career, I was seeking feedback from my supervisor about my strengths, opportunities, and career trajectory. What he shared was a bit surprising. He informed me, "Some of your peers think you can come across as cocky or arrogant." While I am confident in my abilities, I was disappointed to hear that my peers used these descriptors. I asked my supervisor for examples of this behavior. What he shared with me was the difference between calm and panicked. He recounted a difficult situation facing the organization. Given the nature of the situation, the team I was leading would carry the bulk of the burden. During the senior leadership meeting in which we were discussing the issue, he looked at me and said, "This is going to be tough, but it's got to be done."

I calmly, and without knowledge of exactly what we would do at that point, responded, "We'll figure it out."

We then went to the next topic of discussion without speculating how bad things might get and without wringing our hands.

After that meeting, he apparently had at least one of my peers complain about my "cocky" response, "We'll figure it out."

Given this was the sole example he was able to provide of my alleged arrogance, I asked, "As you outlined the issue, would they have preferred I curled up in a fetal position under the table?" Additionally, I shared an experience with him that left an indelible impression on me. During one football practice in college, we were installing a new blitz package for my position to rush the quarterback in the event the opposing team ran a pass play with a specific formation. I will never forget our defensive coordinator grabbing my facemask, pulling me close, and in a calm monotone voice telling me, "If we call this and they throw the ball, I need you to get to the quarterback so my kids can eat."

"Yes, sir!" I replied.

In the pursuit of a higher standard, especially during a crisis, there is no room for excuses. If you create room, you effectively lower the bar. In that moment of concession, you have told yourself and the rest of the organization that something less than our best will be acceptable. What a shame for you, your team, and your customers!

The winning mentality in calm or chaos is well documented in the poem by Walter D. Wintle, "The Man Who Thinks He Can":

> If you think you are beaten, you are;
> If you think you dare not, you don't.
> If you'd like to win, but think you can't,
> It is almost a cinch that you won't.
>
> If you think you'll lose, you've lost;
> For out in this world we find
> Success begins with a fellow's will
> It's all in the state of mind.
>
> If you think you're outclassed, you are;
> You've got to think high to rise.
> You've got to be sure of yourself before
> You can ever win the prize.
>
> Life's battles don't always go
> To the stronger or faster man;
> But sooner or later the person who wins
> Is the one who thinks he can!

At the onset of the pandemic, had we panicked or trembled in fear, I cannot imagine what that would have done to the morale of our team or the outcomes of our patients. At the writing of this book, we are still in the pandemic, but our team is now managing as a daily activity that which was foreign to us early on.

Pause and Reflect

No situation or solution is going to be perfect. There will always be opportunities for improvement. With that in mind, always be mindful of self-doubt. It can be a killer in future decision making and strategic execution.

A young executive I have mentored for over a decade was recently struggling with self-doubt. He is truly a great leader, yet he was struggling even though his company was growing and thriving under his leadership. I challenged him to reflect on the financial analyst position he was in when we first met. Then I challenged him to reflect on all the great decisions he had made over the past decade to become the founder of his own company.

There were plenty of poor decisions and moments of weak execution. Yet all of those were overshadowed by countless victories and great decisions that were spot on given the dynamics. He had also made several terrific hires that propelled the company forward. Within a few moments of our conversation, his entire attitude changed about the future—simply by pausing to reflect on where he had been, the progress required to reach his current milestone, and more importantly, the heights to which he aspires.

Yes, self-doubt can be a mental cancer, but you can typically crush self-doubt by taking a moment to pause and reflect on the journey that brought you to your current state while becoming invigorated about the future.

One thing is certain: humility coupled with intentionality will take you much further than fretting over a situation or commiserating around (or under) a conference table.

LEADERSHIP LESSON

Leading in and through crises demands a high degree of willingness to deal with uncomfortable, often foreign situations. You should never fall into the leadership trap of believing you must have all the answers; you never will. The sooner you realize that the better off you, and the people in your care, will be. Instead, know in your heart, "We will figure it out." What does that look like in operational terms?

1) Rely on teamwork.
2) Assess the variables.
3) Develop the best plan possible.
4) Execute as if your next breath depended on it.
5) Reassess your effectiveness in the most appropriately brief time cycles possible.
6) If outcomes are headed in the right direction, keep going; if not, go back to step 2.

Never Stop Leading

A few years ago, our family had just returned from a fishing trip on a Sunday afternoon. I received one of the most startling text messages of my life. The notification informed everyone on the distribution list that there was a gunman in our Emergency Department. The Special Weapons and Tactics Team was on the way.

The gunman entered the hospital with two small children in tow. Waving a gun, he was demanding to see a patient who was not at our facility. Thanks to the quick thinking of a seasoned nurse, she asked for permission to take the children to a quiet room while simultaneously instructing the few visitors and patients in the waiting area to exit the building. By the time I received the call, the gunman was isolated in the waiting area.

At this point, I threw on a company logo shirt and headed toward the hospital. My wife and son expressed concern about my desire to be onsite. I assured them that professionals were dealing with the gunman. I was not going to charge in and take a bullet trying to "save the day." My concern was for our team in the building.

Upon arrival to our campus, I went to the checkpoint to identify myself. The officer in charge allowed me to enter our Emergency Department through a back door. What I saw upon entry was an amazing care team still delivering care during one of the most stressful experiences of their career. All patients who could be moved were huddled in a hallway at the furthest point away from the gunman, intravenous drips still flowing. While visiting with patients and family members, it was clear they were grateful for our team and the leadership they were displaying in the moment.

Shortly after checking on our team and patients, my role shifted to working with the SWAT commander providing information on the layout of the department, potential gas lines, etc.—all in the interest of identifying "shooting lanes." It was a surreal moment when the commander said shooting lanes in reference to our Emergency Department. I thought to myself,

This isn't a gun range! This is a hospital! Nonetheless, that was the reality of our situation.

Thankfully, after a few hours, the man surrendered his gun. The only injury was sustained by one of our security officers during the scuffle to handcuff the gunman. So much could have gone wrong if not for the bravery and clear thinking of several individuals.

Amid the chaos, a profound example of leadership was witnessed that day. During this particular shift, two physicians were covering our Emergency Department. As soon as the gunman was announced, Dr. Dustin Corgan immediately jumped into action, coordinating our team and the care needed for our patients. The other physician fled to a secured room on the other side of the campus. While I do not fault the physician who ran, I was and remain overwhelmingly impressed by Dr. Corgan's leadership. He stayed and assumed responsibility for the entire Emergency Department during the three-hour ordeal. Even as I was moving about the department, I noticed several times how he interacted with our team or patients, providing direction and answering questions with the calmest demeanor as if it was a normal Sunday afternoon.

After the gunman was taken into custody, I felt compelled to ask Dr. Corgan, "When your colleague ran away, why did you stay?"

His response was simple yet revealing: "Our patients still needed care. The team still needed me."

That type of brave leadership is something to which we should all aspire. It would have been easy to abandon ship, but love compels us to higher standards. Dr. Corgan's actions were clearly uncommon and caring. For his valor, he was honored as the Physician of the Year by the Dallas-Fort Worth Hospital Council.

LEADERSHIP LESSON

As much as we might train for it, crises are as unique as human beings. We can never be fully prepared for what we may face nor how those around us may react. The duty of a loving leader is to reassure people in that moment, provide direction, and stay focused on how to best care for your team and customers in the midst of chaos.

17
LOVE: THE GREATEST MULTIPLIER

Love is the gift that multiplies when given.
—Susan Winter

In a world of what-have-you-done-for-me-lately, it is incredibly easy to become fixated on metrics and trend charts and lose sight of how success is ultimately achieved—through people. I have worked with several leaders who spend extraordinary amounts of time and effort to move whatever needle they are chasing at the time and spend far less time focused on developing people who can make an impact. While organizations can experience temporary improvements with this approach, when trend charts are prioritized over people, the success will be short-lived.

Seeing Is Believing

As mentioned earlier, the first organization I served as president was in the process of opening a replacement facility before I arrived. There was a lot of excitement. Six months before we moved into the new facility, we initiated an extreme focus on our team's well-being. The old facility was small enough that I could visit each inpatient daily. While doing so, I was able to visit with the team and get to know them better. Initially, there was strong concern and people asking, "Why is the president walking around the hospital talking to people?" One caregiver mentioned, "I've been here for years and the only time I've ever seen the president is when we did something wrong." What an unfortunate experience. In a short period of time, our team became accustomed to regular interactions with me.

During the time out in the hospital, I was also able to set the tone that leadership is about service to others. If a leader claims to love and care for their team but the team never sees them, success is going to be scarce. On the other hand, meaningful interactions focused on figuring out how to serve can make a big impact.

In no time at all, we were set to move into the new facility. As a team, we frequently discussed how this was a tremendous opportunity to make a great first impression on the communities we served. Many experts suggested we might experience 5 percent growth in the first year and would decline to a more organic market growth rate thereafter. Again, given the expenses of opening a new facility in an existing market, those same experts predicted we would lose over eleven million dollars in year one with the hope of being at break-even by year five.

As it turned out, year one was a flurry of getting settled into the new facility and keeping up with tremendous growth. The predicted 5 percent in year one turned into an actual growth rate of more than 20 percent. In addition to narrowly generating a positive bottom line in the face of huge expected losses, we saw increases in many other key metrics.

Another incredibly important change took place in our collective mindset. At the old facility when performance was suffering, the common excuse was that because our population size was too small, we would not recover if we had one bad outcome. To which I replied, "Then let us make each event a great one, and when we move into the new hospital, we will fix the population size with tremendous growth!" We had to change the way we accepted failure as inevitable. Don't get me wrong, we are all going to fail at something sometime. They key is to never get comfortable with failure.

Year one was an incredible experience. Quality scores sored, patient satisfaction improved, finances made huge strides, and, more importantly, our team member engagement was in the top decile of the nation. Moreover, while we saw tremendous gains in finances, we rarely spoke of finances. Our focus was on loving one another, our patients, and their families.

The next three years were much the same as year one. Historically, we saw 80 percent of our business come from within a fifteen-minute radius of our facility. Over the course of four years of double-digit annual growth that radius grew to forty-five minutes.

Stay Focused

The word was out, and people loved what we were providing. During one board of directors meeting, a member of our board asked about pursuing a prestigious national quality award. I knew this would involve paying a fee, hiring a consultant, spending a lot of resources, and writing an application in hopes of winning a trophy. Having a strong familiarity with the process, I tried to redirect the board member with two points. First, in over twenty years of healthcare experience, I was not aware of one instance of a patient entering a hospital and asking to see the trophy case before care could be rendered. Second, I would much rather redirect the resource consumption to the bedside in hopes that people chasing trophies would end up calling us to see how we are achieving the outcomes we are producing.

Similarly, as we grew, a competitor leased a billboard that was located adjacent to our campus. This irritated a number of people on our team. My encouragement was to stay focused on what we control—world-class patient care. Eventually, the competitor must have realized the billboard was a waste of money, so it again became available. I received several phone calls and text messages hoping we would seize the opportunity to lease the billboard. My response to each urging was the same. First, how many people do you know who make healthcare decisions based upon billboards? The answer was typically zero. Second, I would rather spend the expense of the billboard at the bedside to further improve our outcomes. Third, our continued growth likely allowed our friendly competitor to see the futility of the billboard. Finally, we had a three-hundred-thousand square foot facility right next to the billboard. I would much prefer we spend our attention and effort focused on how we get better each day than chasing billboards.

As a result of creating a loving culture and staying focused, our facility became nationally recognized for top decile outcomes in three short years.

Without a strong focus on finances, our culture and high expectations around caring for one another inherently created an organization that became financially strong. Two different colleagues approached me during our remarkable growth with the same statement: "You guys are printing money, aren't you!"

They struggled to respond when I told each of them: "No. We're just trying to love people."

During this same time, the experts who by and large created our budget target would routinely accuse us of sandbagging on our budgets, even though they were the ones who created our budget targets.

Let's Do This Again

The second hospital where I served as president was a similar story, even though the market dynamics were considerably different. This market had much greater population density, but it was also overrun with competitors. One day I asked a newcomer, "As a start-up, are you concerned with market saturation?"

He responded, "Given this market, we can see a very small number of patients and still break even." That attitude seemed to resonate with many other organizations, and competitors kept coming.

Nonetheless, within the span of two years, we had become a nationally recognized hospital for quality of care, patient satisfaction, and efficient and effective care. Again, without a heavy focus on finances, our earnings increased 50 percent in two years and that despite our presence in an incredibly competitive and mature market. While growth was slower in this second example, we still grew. The bigger opportunity that was less prominent than in the first hospital was the opportunity to improve the efficiency and effectiveness of our care.

We shared a statistic with our team related to loving our patients. According to United States Courts, a government website, several hundred thousand families file for bankruptcy each year.[6] We would always ask, "Does anyone know the number one cause for these bankruptcies?" Typically, 90 percent of the audience would respond, "Healthcare bills." They were right.

One way we can demonstrate love for our patients is to ensure that, before they are discharged and begin to receive their medical bills, we (1) provide the right care at the right time, (2) return them to a state of health as quickly as possible so they can return home, and (3) deliver care in such a way that they do not end up back in the hospital because of a rebound illness. This focus led us to become much more skilled at eliminating waste in our processes, not so the hospital could make more money but to allow our patients to receive outstanding care without it becoming a crippling financial burden. Over time, this became a discipline that was applied to everything we did without the focus being "We have to cut so many millions of dollars because we are performing poorly on financial statements."

The other fundamental concept of allowing love to be your multiplier is something I learned in my first six months working as a management engineer straight out of college—namely, the people closest to the work have the best ideas for making life better. It is not some genius in the corner office, certainly not some engineer straight out of college, but rather the people grinding on the front lines who have great ideas on how to provide better services and eliminate roadblocks to excellence. If you develop a trusting relationship based on how you care for people personally or professionally, you will be able to get so much more accomplished.

Unfortunately, love does not fit well in most financial equations. Love is not a natural variable in a pro forma or spreadsheet, but it is without question a multiplier.

LEADERSHIP LESSON

Never underestimate the power of love to improve and grow whatever it touches.

Most of us were never taught about love in school. Hopefully, our parents or some other influential figure in our lives explained the concept, but even then, it is rarely applied to what we do for a living. Business leaders especially are not taught the multiplying ability love can have on a group of people. Instead, we are taught to focus on that which we can concretely measure. Endless possibilities are lost with this fixed mindset.

Commit yourself to pursuing the opportunities that lie beyond traditional business wisdom. Make yours a loving environment, and watch people grow.

18

LOVE NEVER FAILS

Love never fails.
—Paul of Tarsus

In our electronic world, it is easy to fall into the trap of instant gratification given how simple our smart phones and vendor service offerings have made life. My wife and I recently placed our first electronic order for groceries and had them delivered directly to our front door within a couple of hours. Something as routine as a smoothie or cup of coffee can be ordered on your phone to avoid the arduous journey of walking into the store and placing an order at the counter. Do not get me wrong, from a process engineering standpoint, the efficiency is a beautiful thing. But I recently witnessed a fellow customer angrily yelling at some poor kids because her order was not ready when she arrived. It is unfair for me to judge her because I do not know the full situation. She could have been dealing with more than she could handle that day, but the way she acted because her order was not immediately ready when she arrived was embarrassing.

The point of sharing that story is to convey our need to be more persistent and resilient as individuals and as a society. Life is not always going to be perfect. The utopian cocoons we attempt to manufacture will inevitably bring disappointments, which are part of life. How we react in moments of difficulty have a huge influence on the world around us.

In the scenario above, as the lady berated the workers because her order was not ready upon her arrival, the workers offered her a full refund if she would leave the store—an offer she accepted. During the back-and-forth, the upset customer periodically looked at me and other customers, trying to gain solidarity among those waiting. No one gave that to her. Instead, several of us thanked the workers for providing the much-desired service, even if we had to wait a little for the fulfillment of our orders.

Persistence and discipline allow us to continue making progress, even when we may not feel terribly motivated. There is so much value in simply showing up on a regular basis. When you string a few days together where your excitement level is not at its peak but you still got out of bed and showed up, you increase your likelihood of seeing progress. One of my favorite things to watch from a leadership perspective is how progress breeds more progress. String progression together and over time you have success.

However, that does not happen if we get frustrated or throw tantrums because something did not happen exactly as we planned it. It is in the moments of disappointment that we grow and foster growth in those around us.

Uncommon Robin

At the first hospital I mentioned in this book, the ambulatory surgery area was known for creating extraordinarily strong patient experiences. They had an amazing leader named Robin McCommons. Through her leadership, the department was at a level where most hospitals would have thrown a party to celebrate the wonderful outcomes. As the entire organization continued to grow relative to our outcomes and expectations, Robin helped her team set a new standard for themselves. They rejected the notion that being near the top decile in the nation was acceptable. Instead, they began to challenge themselves to be better.

Occasionally they would see a particular month's performance struggle per their new standards. When this would happen, it was like a five-alarm fire for her team. During these occasional performance troughs, she and her team would dive deep into the data to figure out what they could have done better or what process changes needed to be implemented. Again, performance that would have generated celebrations at many organizations became almost detestable for Robin and her team. Performing at the 90th percentile in the nation became a disappointment because of the persistence they demonstrated around the pursuit of perfection.

As time went on and they remained dedicated to their efforts, they grew to know and exemplify the persistence required by our friend and focus: excellence. To be clear, they were operating in a highly competitive environment when aiming for excellence in ambulatory surgery patient experience. Nonetheless, in a relatively short time frame, they received the Press Ganey Guardian of Excellence Award for performing at or above the 95th percentile in the nation related to patient experience for an entire year.

This persistent thirst for excellence began to infiltrate other areas of the organization. Robin and her team were exemplars. They had no secret, no silver bullet. But they had persistence by the truckloads. In what seemed like no time at all, they received their second consecutive Guardian of Excellence Award and then their third and then their fourth. This team went from consistently good to perpetual excellence by changing their mindset about what was acceptable and displaying a persistence that truly is the price of admission to excellence. The impact this group had on the entire hospital, and other hospitals for that matter, cannot be overstated. They repeatedly demonstrated that the seemingly unattainable can be achieved through a very disciplined and persistent focus on a lofty goal.

Robin's team achieved these extraordinary results from a simple yet elegant approach. First, they changed their mental reality in terms of what they aspired to be; this was foundational. Next, they conveyed the vision of excellence to their entire team. In parallel, while gaining momentum with their vision, they began deep analytics relative to their performance and their processes. They had bedside leaders driving ownership of data realities as well as ideas on how to address deficiencies. It was truly an honor to watch this take place. You could walk into any sub-department of this area and people knew what their patients thought of them as well as what they were doing to get better—even while taking up permanent residence at the 95th percentile!

This became a way of life for Robin's team. It was an iterative process that literally anyone can follow with the right mindset and the will to be great.

The diagram below helps illustrate this process:

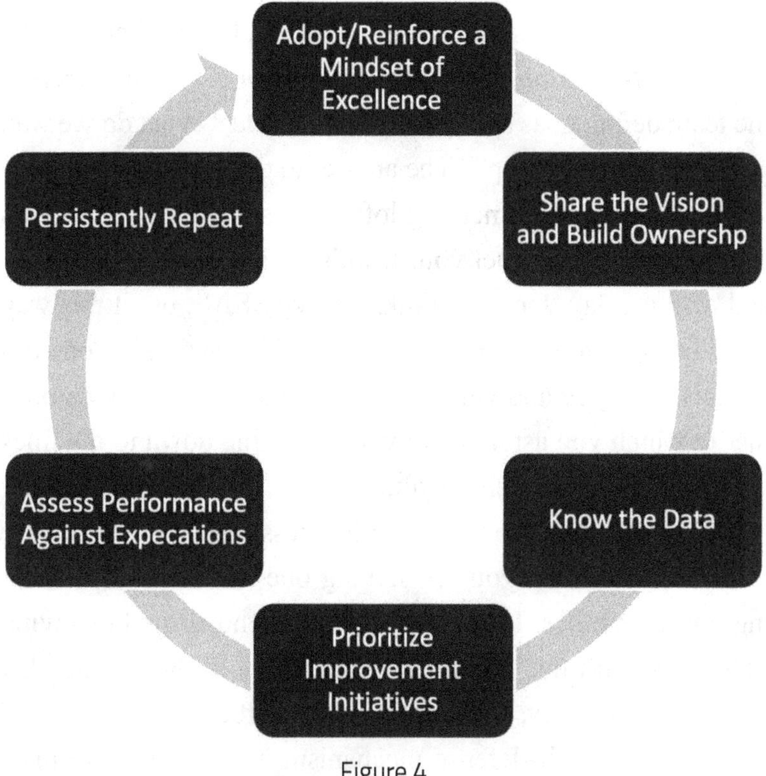

Figure 4

Adopting and reinforcing a mindset of excellence involves an inherent desire to bring your best every day in every situation, while working daily to improve your best. Regardless of the successes, and there will be plenty, you must maintain a humble attitude knowing you and the world around you can always be better. Regardless of the mediocrity or even failure you and your team may be experiencing, know that nothing remains the same. Change is expected. It is a way a life—no exceptions. Anticipate it with a fervor that propels you into the change itself, into progress. "Average" should become an offensive ideology. My experience has shown this mindset is best accomplished if you have a group of people who love one another and love what they do.

Share the vision and build ownership entails members of the team defining, as specifically as possible, "What do we want to be when we grow up?" The answer to that question should be something special, something lofty, and something uncommon. That answer should fuel your team's desire to get up, show up, and own the day. Jocco Willink, a Navy SEAL, put it this way: "You must own everything in your world. There is no one else to blame." If you and your entire team adopt a shared vision of that to which you aspire and own everything down to the finest details, you will be well on your way to achieving that vision.

Know the data requires a willingness and sense of security to be real with how you are serving one another and performing on key metrics. I have a dear friend who is fond of saying, "The data don't lie." Similarly, legendary NFL head coach Bill Parcells used to say, "You are what your record says you are." Routinely as a self-defense mechanism, we are prone to make excuses or justify why we are doing well when we are not. The best gift we can ever give ourselves is an appreciation for and a grasp on reality. If there is a larger than desired gap between where you are and your aspiration, become comfortable with that tension but do not explain it away. Through deep dives into data, know your strengths and weaknesses. Embrace both, but do not waste time trying to justify weaknesses. Instead, know that data and get to work.

Prioritizing improvement initiatives allows us to plan our work in order to work our plan. Depending upon the degree of improvement needed, I am a big fan of the Dave Ramsey approach to debt reduction: focus on small wins and allow that momentum to carry you onto bigger wins. The more daunting the improvement gap, the greater the energy, and potentially political capital will be required to scale the peak. If possible, avoid selecting Mount Everest as your top priority. Start with something that prepares you for Everest, knowing Everest is the ultimate goal. As you check off smaller wins, be certain to celebrate wins with your team. It will be food for their soul as you implement this approach in your journey to excellence.

Assessing performance against expectations seems benign, but here is where many efforts and organizations go adrift. We put so much effort into pursuing our goals. We become so desperate to celebrate something that we compromise our constitution and prematurely proclaim victory. It is like running the first twenty-four miles of a marathon and deciding, "That's good enough." That mindset will get you a one-way ticket to pursuing standards set by others who are unwilling to compromise. Much like *knowing the data*, take an honest look when assessing actual performance against expectations and never sell yourself, your team, or your customers short. Hopefully, you and your team have achieved your goal and are ready to move onto the next big goal. If not, you will need to determine why you failed to achieve your desired outcomes and set a course for future success. A word of encouragement: embrace this pressure, embrace the struggle. This is where you and your team will grow stronger if you are persistent in your aspirations for excellence.

Persistently repeating this process and *reinforcing a mindset of excellence* becomes a lifestyle, a never-ending pursuit of a higher standard. Much like *assessing performance against expectations*, there is a danger in this step of taking the off -ramp to complacency. Historic success can be a great deterrent to future success. It is easy to become so intoxicated with victories that we begin to slumber, assuming success will continue on its own. Undoubtedly success creates momentum for future successes but only if properly nurtured and cared for. Therefore, we must *persistently repeat* the process that created the victories. Each iteration will require a renewed sense of purpose and determination. Every day you, as the leader, must create a renewed sense of urgency—a revived focus on why we cannot be satisfied with where we are, and why we must leave the comforts rightfully earned by our accomplishments so we can set a higher standard. From this perspective, there can be no plan B.

In a budget review meeting not long ago, we were faced with an ever-increasing demand. Our team laid out our plan of attack and were asked, "What is your plan B if that does not work?" Our plan B was to revisit our execution on plan A and determine if there might be alternative strategies we should employ. This approach accomplishes two things:

1) It develops commitment to the agreed upon plan.
2) It prevents chasing less optimal strategies that will only waste time or detract from Plan A.

People will always second-guess you if you fail to meet objectives. Sometimes they will even take joy in your failure if you have a track record of success. You must become comfortable with uncomfortable situations and remember that opinions are not facts. Typically, opinions are the lowest form of information and reflect underlying issues of the owner. That said, remain humble and receive feedback. Stay focused on the execution of plan A, and remember that love always demands our best.

LEADERSHIP LESSON

Have a plan. Work that plan. Do not be afraid to alter your plan but remain persistent in your commitment and execution. Whether you are experiencing successes or failures, the one thing a loving culture requires is dogmatic follow-through and follow-up to ensure execution and outcomes are consistently moving in the right direction.

What Matters Most

Your leadership is the antidote to average! You can be tempted by the allure of chasing trophies. You can focus on the demands and pressure associated with better performance and upward reaching trend lines. While there is nothing wrong with achieving these things, always remember that they are by-products of the process of loving people. Many organizations will mistakenly make the trend charts and trophies their priority. In the process, they will inevitably devalue people. This fatal flaw will create a much more challenging road on the journey to excellence. If, however, we prioritize loving people, all these other things, the by-products, will be added to our life.

In parting, I would like to share some of my greatest professional treasures. These are my "trophies." They are some of the comments I've received over the years that show what love can do when it's the standard to which you aspire. I do not share these sentiments as a means of boasting, but as a point of reflection on what is most important—loving and serving those with whom we labor.

> "I am honored and humbled to have called this my home for one year now! What a blessing it and you are in my life. Thank you for the role model you are. The calm you exhibit. The loyalty you instill. And the humor you bring. Thank you for the value you see and develop in others. I'm running out of room, but I'll never run out of gratitude."

> "How do I begin . . . you have been such an inspiration to me, and I thank God for your leadership. Never in my 25 years have I had this kind of support from my president. Thank you for just 'being real' and loving us all through our mess and pushing us to greatness!"

> "Thank you for changing our hospital to focus on compassionate care. That has always been our calling, but now we have the opportunity to be a place where that happens!"

> "Thank you for being a hands-on president! Interacting with us really means a lot! The candy on Christmas when you could have been home with your family.

The roses on Valentine's Day. Excellent little touches that show you care about us. Thank you for being an excellent president."

"Thank you for taking the time to check on me after a difficult shift. It meant so much to me!"

"I wanted to say thank you for your leadership. I have been here for six months now and wanted you to know how much I have come to admire your leadership and the grace you portray daily. You are more than just a leader to me; you are truly an inspiration. I feel very blessed to come to work here. Your enthusiasm, the culture you promote, and the support make it a pleasure to come to work every day."

"Thank you for making these crazy times feel a little closer to normal. You lead our team with such poise and grace that it is easy to want to come to work. You are visible and approachable for us to speak with you. You never take us for granted and you stand up for us like a parent would stick up for their child. You do this with so little effort that I can tell this is just how you are in everyday life."

"I love the way you lead! The peace around you is contagious during this storm. Thank you for all that you are! Such gratitude as I wipe the tears from my face."

Blessings to *you* on *your* journey! May love for one another be the foundation for the relationships, families, departments, and organizations you are called to build.

ACKNOWLEDGMENTS

There are many people I would like to acknowledge.

Ultimately, I thank God for placing me on this unexpected journey and for all the amazing people who have intersected my path.

To my two great mentors, the late George D. Rise and Reverend Erie Chapman, both of whom were foundational to my life and contributed mightily to the person I am today.

Rami Almutadi, Trish Green, LaKisha Howard, and Keith Nichols—you are all a tremendous blessing in my life. That sentiment was on full display during the writing of this book. Thank you.

Jenni Robbins of Ignite Development, Morgan James Publishing, and editor Bill Watkins—you have made this dream a reality. For each of your instrumental roles, you have my deepest gratitude.

Finally, to all of the team members who suggested this book be written, I thank you for your encouragement and partnership.

ABOUT THE AUTHOR

Chris York has been a dedicated servant leader for thirty years. His leadership experience has been marked by progressively increasing responsibilities and consistently improved performance for a host of hospitals and healthcare systems.

Chris is passionate about driving excellence through a culture based upon (1) love for one another, (2) receiving feedback as a precious gift, and (3) courageously leading change that drives continuous improvement. Through the application of his unique philosophy, multiple hospitals have been recognized nationally for their high quality of care and creation of a Five Star experience.

He is a Fellow of the American College of Healthcare Executives and serves on the board of various community organizations. During the first fifteen years of his career, Chris was bi-vocational and served as a part-time youth minister. He received a football scholarship to attend East Tennessee State University where he earned his undergraduate degree in business administration. He later received his MBA from ETSU, with an emphasis in healthcare administration.

ENDNOTES

1 Frank Outlaw, as quoted in "What They're Saying," *San Antonio Light*, May 18, 1977, 7-B. This quotation is attributed to a number of different people. For an exploration of this, see the Quote Investigator, accessed July 28, 2021, https://quoteinvestigator.com/2013/01/10/watch-your-thoughts/.

2 Miles Burke, "Six Proven Benefits of Engaged Employees and Why This Matters," accessed October 12, 2021, https://inside.6q.io/benefits-of-engaged-employees/.

3 The updated edition of this book is by Joseph Greeny, Kerry Patterson, Ron McMillan, Al Switzler, and Emily Gregory, *Crucial Conversations: Tools for Talking When Stakes Are High*, 3rd ed. (New York: McGraw-Hill Education, 2021).

4 Occupational Safety and Health Administration, "Workplace Violence in Healthcare: Understanding the Challenge," accessed March 14, 2021, https://www.osha.gov/sites/default/files/OSHA3826.pdf.

5 What the Bible actually forbade in the Law of Moses was Israelites marrying Canaanites or any other foreign people who adhered to religious beliefs or moral practices that the Law condemned, such as polygamy, polytheism, and idolatry (Exodus 34:14–16; Deuteronomy 7:3–6). But nowhere does the Bible forbid relationships between people because of their ethnicity, skin color, or race. In fact, in the Hebrew Scriptures, ethnic and national boundaries were often crossed to marry (e.g., Genesis 38:2–6; 41:44–45; Exodus 2:16–21). And in the Christian Scriptures, the apostle Paul says that the cultural disunity between such groups as male and female, slave and free, and Jew and Greek (which included all non-Jews) are dissolved in Christ. These groups have been united and reconciled and now possess equal standing with one another as members in the same Christian community, the body of Christ. For more on such matters, see Richard N. Longenecker, *New Testament Ethics for Today* (Grand Rapids, MI: William B. Eerdmans, 1984); Dave Unander, *Shattering the Myth of Race: Genetic Realities and Biblical Truths* (Valley Forge, PA: Judson Press, 2000), especially ch. 9; H. W. Perkin, "Marriage, Marriage Customs in Bible Times," in the *Evangelical Dictionary of Theology*, ed. Walter A. Elwell (Grand Rapids, MI: Baker Book House, 1984), 690–91; and "Intermarriage, Racial," in the *Encyclopedia of Biblical and Christian Ethics*, gen. ed. R. K. Harrison (Nashville, TN: Thomas Nelson, 1987), 203–204.

6 See, for example, United States Courts, "Annual Bankruptcy Filings Fall 29.7 Percent," January 28, 2021,

updated March 5, 2021, https://www.uscourts.gov/news/2021/01/28/annual-bankruptcy-filings-fall-297-percent; Mark P. Cussen, "Top 5 Reasons Why People Go Bankrupt," Investopedia, updated February 24, 2020, https://www.investopedia.com/financial-edge/0310/top-5-reasons-people-go-bankrupt.aspx; and Lorie Konish, "This Is the Real Reason Most Americans File for Bankruptcy," February 11, 2019, https://www.cnbc.com/2019/02/11/this-is-the-real-reason-most-americans-file-for-bankruptcy.html.